John the I

His life, teaching and impact

By Michael Penny

C000046015

ISBN 978 1 78364 647 0

First edition: published in 2021

Printed in the UK

www.obt.org.uk

****

THE OPEN BIBLE TRUST
Fordland Mount, Upper Basildon,
Reading, RG8 8LU, UK.

John the Baptist

His life, teaching and impact

Contents

Introduction

The last book of the Old Testament, in both time and position, is that of the prophet Malachi, and his closing words are:

> "Behold, I will send you Elijah the prophet before the great and awesome day of the LORD comes. And he will turn the hearts of fathers to their children and the hearts of children to their fathers, lest I come and strike the land with a decree of utter destruction." (Malachi 4:5-6)

This type of two-edged prophecy – of future blessings or future judgment – was a recurring one in the Old Testament. Indeed, Moses stated that for obedience Israel would be blessed, but for disobedience there would be judgments, which could end with the nation being conquered and scattered.

> "And if you faithfully obey the voice of the LORD your God, being careful to do all his commandments that I command you today, the LORD your God will set you high above all the nations of the earth. And all these blessings shall come upon you and overtake you, if you obey the voice of the LORD your God." (Deuteronomy 28:1-2)

> "But if you will not obey the voice of the LORD your God or be careful to do all his commandments and his statutes that I command you today, then all these curses shall come upon you and overtake you." (Deuteronomy 28:15)

> "And the LORD will scatter you among all peoples, from one end of the earth to the other." (Deuteronomy 28:64)

This was not vindictiveness on the part of God, but these were signs[1], to guide the people of Israel (Deuteronomy 28:46), and we see this in much of the Old Testament. For example, Isaiah also warned:

> "If you are willing and obedient, you shall eat the good of the land; but if you refuse and rebel, you shall be eaten by the sword." (Isaiah 1:19-20)

Although in the short-term the people of Israel were obedient to Isaiah's call, after Isaiah's death they fell into idolatry and disobedience and, following various warning judgments, the Babylonians came and conquered the nation, destroying Jerusalem and the temple, and scattering those who survived throughout their empire. So, Jews reading those words of Malachi should have appreciated the background to his closing statement.

However, following Malachi there were some 400 years of chequered history on the part of Israel during which God was silent. There was no word from Him, no warning from heaven, and seemingly no divine action, until the Angel Gabriel appeared on the scene.

Surprisingly, perhaps, the history of the New Testament does not open with Gabriel visiting Mary in Galilee and telling her she is to be the mother of the Son of God. Rather we see Gabriel in Jerusalem, in the temple, telling an old priest, Zechariah, that in their old age he and his wife are to have a son, who is to go before the Lord "in the spirit and power of Elijah" (Luke 1:17).

---

[1] For more on this see *Deuteronomy 28: A Key to Understanding* by Michael Penny published by The Open Bible Trust.

An Air of Expectation

In the pages of the Four Gospels it is easy for us to miss the air of expectation there was in Israel at that time. We can see this with such seemingly ordinary people such as Simeon and Anna. We read that he was a righteous and devout man who was "*waiting* for the consolation of Israel" and it had been revealed to Simeon that he would not die before he had seen the Lord's Christ (Luke 2:26-27). And Anna, having seen the infant Jesus in the temple, began speaking "to **all** who were *waiting* for the redemption of Jerusalem" (Luke 2:38).

Then, years later, we see the leaders in Israel, who knew their Scriptures and who were aware of what should happen before the Messiah appeared, asking John such questions as "Are you Elijah?" (John 1:21). And many of the people in Israel, when asked who they thought Jesus was, had various views: "Some say John the Baptist, others say Elijah, and others Jeremiah or one of the prophets" (Matthew 16:14). And the disciples, who at that point of time were not so learned, asked the Lord "Why do the scribes say Elijah must come first?" (Matthew 17:10).

So why was there such an air of expectation at that time?

Prophetic Background

Earlier I mentioned the judgment that befell the Jews at the hands of the Babylonians. Jeremiah had earlier prophesied some details of this future captivity:

> "This whole land shall become a ruin and a waste, and these nations shall serve the king of Babylon seventy years. Then after seventy years are completed, I will punish the king of

Babylon and that nation, the land of the Chaldeans, for their iniquity, declares the Lord, making the land an everlasting waste" ... "For thus says the Lord: When seventy years are completed for Babylon, I will visit you, and I will fulfil to you my promise and bring you back to this place." (Jeremiah 25:11-12; 29:10)

Years after Jeremiah had written this, and the Jews were languishing in Babylon, we read that Daniel had a copy of the scroll of the prophet Jeremiah.

In the first year of his [Darius] reign, I, Daniel, perceived in the books the number of years that, according to the word of the Lord to Jeremiah the prophet, must pass before the end of the desolations of Jerusalem, namely, seventy years. (Daniel 9:2)

Those seventy years were coming to an end and there must have been, amongst the Jewish community in Babylon, an air of expectancy about what was soon to happen. However, Daniel himself received a prophecy from Gabriel with a fixed period of time as to when it would come about.

"Seventy weeks are decreed about your people and your holy city, to finish the transgression, to put an end to sin, and to atone for iniquity, to bring in everlasting righteousness, to seal both vision and prophet, and to anoint a most holy place. Know therefore and understand that from the going out of the word to restore and build Jerusalem to the coming of an anointed one, a prince, there shall be seven weeks. Then for sixty-two weeks it shall be built again with squares and moat, but in a troubled time. And after the sixty-two weeks, an anointed one shall be cut off and shall have nothing." (Daniel 9:24-26)

Now none of this happened within seventy literal 'weeks' and the footnote in the *ESV* has 'seventy *sevens*', which is how it is translated in many version (e.g. NIV, NRSV, NASB, KJV). And this expression refers to seventy weeks of years, or seventy sevens of years; i.e. 490 years. And after sixty-two sevens of years (i.e. 434) Gabriel said there was to be a significant event, an anointed one was to be cut off.

The exact meaning of this prophecy is open to debate, as is its timing.[2] However, it seems that when we open the pages of the New Testament, the years mentioned in this prophecy were ticking away. Like Daniel, who understood from reading Jeremiah that the time was approaching when the Jews would return to Jerusalem, some in New Testament times, from the reading of Daniel, knew that the time was approaching for the fulfilment of what Daniel wrote about. This contributed to the air of expectation.

Also, when the wise men visited Herod they asked "Where is he who has been born King of the Jews?" (Matthew 2:2). Herod discussed this with the chief priests and scribes, who probably deduced that He would commence His ministry when an adult. This may also have contributed to the air of expectancy.

So, returning to Malachi, the Old Testament closed with the two-edged prophecy. Would there be blessings for the nation or judgment? What was going to happen? The answer lies in the pages of the New Testament.

---

[2] For more on this see *Daniel's Seventy Sevens: A Recalculation* by Michael Penny published by The Open Bible Trust.

Chapter 1

The Visit of the Angel Gabriel

The Future Parents

> In the days of Herod, king of Judea, there was a priest named Zechariah, of the division of Abijah. And he had a wife from the daughters of Aaron, and her name was Elizabeth. And they were both righteous before God, walking blamelessly in all the commandments and statutes of the Lord. But they had no child, because Elizabeth was barren, and both were advanced in years. (Luke 1:5-7)

Being a priest, Zechariah was a descendant of Aaron, as all priests had to be, and so, too, was his wife. Their predicament was not dissimilar to that of Abraham and Sarah who had not been able to have children either, until God worked a miracle in their old age (Genesis 17).

> Now while he [Zechariah] was serving as priest before God when his division was on duty, according to the custom of the priesthood, he was chosen by lot to enter the temple of the Lord and burn incense. And the whole multitude of the people were praying outside at the hour of incense. (Luke 1:8-10)

The priests were divided into twenty-four divisions and Abijah was the eighth (1 Chronicles 24:10). Most of the year they served out in the community. However, for two weeks each year they were in Jerusalem to serve in the temple and perform various duties, some of which were allocated by the casting of lots. On this occasion, the lot fell on Zechariah to burn incense. This was a great privilege.[3] However, when we read the word 'temple' in the New Testament we need to be careful.

Sometimes it refers to the whole building, including the outer porches (or porticos) and the Court of the Gentiles. At other times it refers to the inner buildings which enclosed the Court of Women, the Court of Men (Israel) and the Court of Priests, etc. No uncircumcised man could enter these areas. However, sometimes it refers to just the building which housed the Holy Place and the Most Holy Place (the Holy of Holies). Only the priests could enter the Holy Place and only the High Priest (just once a year on the Day of Atonement) could enter the Most Holy Place. The images shown next depict what the buildings may have looked like.

---

[3] "As there were so many priests, it was not allowed that a priest should burn incense more than once in his lifetime." (Norval Geldenhuys, *The New London Commentary on the New Testament: The Gospel of Luke*, page 62).

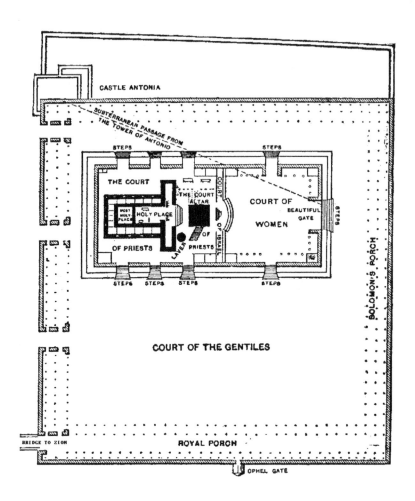

Now the Altar of Incense was located in the Holy Place, as the next diagram shows, and so, as mentioned, Zechariah was greatly privileged to have this duty to perform. However, it should not have taken him long to have lit the incense and set it burning but, as we shall see, those waiting outside grew concerned about him for he was in the Holy Place much longer than they had anticipated.

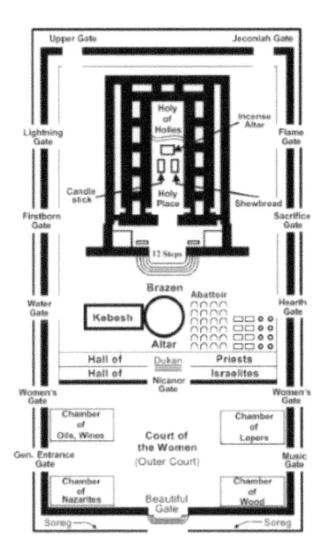

Zechariah and the Angel Gabriel

Luke praises both Zechariah and Elizabeth, saying of them that "they were both righteous before God, walking blamelessly in all the commandments and statutes of the Lord" (Luke 1:6). That being the case, one can imagine that Zechariah, with great humility, entered the Holy Place and passed the Table of Shewbread on his right and the Golden Candlestick on his left. Ahead of him was the Altar of Incense. We are not told whether or not he had lit the incense before he noticed someone, a man[4], standing to the right of the Altar. This would have surprised and shocked him.

> And there appeared to him an angel of the Lord standing on the right side of the altar of incense. And Zechariah was troubled when he saw him, and fear fell upon him. But the angel said to him, "Do not be afraid …" (Luke 1:11-13)

In fact, more than being simply surprised and shocked, Zechariah was troubled – there should have been no-one else in there! – and fearful – what was this person doing in there? The initial reaction of the angel was to ease Zechariah's fear, to calm him for what he was about to be told.

> "Zechariah … your prayer has been heard, and your wife Elizabeth will bear you a son, and you shall call his name John. And you will have joy and gladness, and many will rejoice at his birth, for he will be great before the Lord. And he must not drink wine or strong drink, and he will be filled with the Holy Spirit, even from his mother's womb. And he will turn many of the children of Israel to the Lord their God, and he will go before him in the spirit and power of Elijah, to turn the hearts of the fathers to the children, and the disobedient to the wisdom of the just, to make ready for the Lord a people prepared." (Luke 1:13-17)

Understandably Zechariah and Elizabeth had been praying for a child for years, and it seems even continued to do so into their old

---

[4] In the Bible angels always appear as men; not beings with wings. So as far as Zechariah was concerned an unknown man was standing there.

age, maybe thinking of Abraham and Sarah. However, on that day he probably would have been praying for his nation, desiring the promised Messiah, who would come and restore the kingdom to Israel. If that were the case, that prayer was answered for the angel announced that they would have a child, a son, a special son, who was to be called John, and who was to be the forerunner to the Messiah.

Naturally they would have joy and gladness, as aged parents who had been unable to have children. Many, especially relatives, would rejoice at the prospect of his birth, but the usual delight and happiness at the birth of a child was *not* what the angel was referring to. Rather the reason that "many will rejoice" was that "he will be great before the Lord" and, following the injunction that he would not drink alcohol, the angel explained how and why this John was to be great.

- He will be filled with the Holy Spirit, even from his mother's womb.
- He will turn many of the children of Israel to the Lord their God.
- He will go before him [the Lord] in the spirit and power of Elijah.
- He will turn the hearts of the fathers to the children, and the disobedient to the wisdom of the just.
- He will make ready for the Lord a people prepared.

Some of what the angel said refers back to what Malachi had written. For example, "He will turn the hearts of fathers to their children" (Malachi 4:6), and he was to prepare the way for the Lord (Malachi 3:1). However, one thing was startlingly different.

He will be filled with the Holy Spirit, even from his mother's womb.

This would have quite amazed Zechariah. Nothing like this had ever happened to anyone before (or since). There are many references in the Old Testament to the Holy Spirit and His work. For example:

> He had come upon people to strengthen them (Judges 14:5-6) and to enable them to do all manner of skilful work (Exodus 28:1-5; 31:1-5). He had given them the ability to prophesy (Numbers 11:24-30), to administer with wisdom (Judges 3:10; 6:34; 11:29; 13:25), and many other talents and skills that they had required. However, He did not abide with them continually. Neither did He indwell them permanently. When their task was over, when their work was completed, He departed and they lost their skills and abilities. (Michael Penny, *The Miracles of the Apostles,* OBT)[5]

So, to hear that his son was to be filled with the Holy Spirit from birth, or possibly even before he had been born – "even from his mother's womb" – would have been amazing … unbelievable!

Two Questions

If we can appreciate just how staggering a statement the angel's words were to Zechariah, it is not surprising that he doubted the possibility of what he had just heard, and that he questioned the truth of what Gabriel had told him. For he and Elizabeth to have a

---

[5] Later, Christ was to promise His disciples that, after He had returned to the Father, they would receive the Spirit who was to remain with them forever – this was new and different. (See John 14:16-17.)

child at their age would require a mighty miracle from God, and perhaps the humility of this righteous man (Luke 1:6) made it even harder to believe that he would be the father of someone so special. Zechariah's words imply that he wanted a sign to confirm the truth of what he had been told[6].

> And Zechariah said to the angel, "How shall I know this? For I am an old man, and my wife is advanced in years." (Luke 1:18)

Clearly the angel was not impressed by this man's attitude and question, for he retorted:

> "I am Gabriel. I stand in the presence of God, and I was sent to speak to you and to bring you this good news. And behold, you will be silent and unable to speak until the day that these things take place, because you did not believe my words, which will be fulfilled in their time." (Luke 1:19-21)

So, Zechariah got his miraculous sign: silence, until the birth of his son.

It is interesting to compare Zechariah's encounter with Gabriel with the angel's visit and annunciation to Mary (Luke 1:26-38). She, too, asked a question: "How can this be, since I am a virgin?" However, it appears this was not a question asked in doubt or disbelief, but was one sparked by a genuine desire to know how this would come about. The angel explained and, in some way,

---

[6] This was not uncommon in the Old Testament. We can think of Gideon's fleece, and others, who asked for a small sign, or miracle, to confirm in their minds that the greater, future promise would come to pass.

gave her a sign that it would happen to her as he had said. He pointed her to her previously barren and aged relative Elizabeth who, by that time, was six months pregnant, and he concluded with the words "For nothing is impossible with God." To which Mary replied, "I am the Lord's servant. May it be to me as you have said."[7]

The ensuing days, weeks and months (Luke 1:21-25)

Generally speaking, the burning of the incense took but a short while, but this encounter with Gabriel meant that Zechariah was in the Holy Place for quite some time. I am sure the discussion between the angel and the man was far more than what Luke has recorded. He recorded just the core of the conversation. But Zechariah was in the Holy Place so long that the temple procedures were held up and those waiting outside, mainly other priests one suspects, were wondering what had delayed him.

Eventually he emerged from the Holy Place and stood at the top of the steps where it was customary for the priest to pronounce the Aaronic blessing of Numbers 6:24-26; but there was just silence. No doubt slowly, the other priests started to question him as to as why he had taken so long, and why hadn't he given the blessing? But they received no reply. They soon realised he was unable to speak and they concluded he had seen a vision.

We know that Zechariah could write (Luke 1:63), but whether or not he wrote that he had seen an angel, we do not know. And if he

---

[7] From these two questions it appears the Lord is happy for us to question Him and Scripture, provided we have a genuine desire to want to know and understand. However, to question with an unbelieving or critical attitude is an entirely different matter.

had, it is perhaps doubtful that he would have told them that Gabriel had said to him that he and Elizabeth were to have a son in their old age. Possibly he feared the people would laugh and scoff, and ridicule him. Maybe he still did not believe what he had been told. However, having been struck dumb as a sign, perhaps he thought the promise was simply too good to be true.

In his mute state, Zechariah completed his two weeks of service and then went home and, one suspects, within a relatively short space of time Elizabeth conceived. However, once she discovered she was pregnant she did not go out in public! One wonders why! Was she, perhaps, anxious that she may lose the baby? Or, being old, she may have found it tiring? Whatever the reason, she rejoiced, praising the Lord and saying, "Thus the Lord has done for me in the days when he looked on me, to take away my reproach among people" (Luke 1:25).

The third trimester is often a difficult and tiring time for any pregnant woman. However, for one as old as Elizabeth, it was going to be particularly problematic; but help was on its way.

A Special Visitor

At the end of his meeting with Mary, Gabriel pointed her to Elizabeth, who was six months pregnant. So, Mary went to see Elizabeth and stayed there for about three months (Luke 1:39,56). Whether this was at the instigation of the angel or just a normal family routine, we do not know. However, it was, and still is in some societies today, typical for a teenage young girl to go and live with a pregnant relative in her last weeks of pregnancy.

When Mary entered the home of Zechariah and greeted Elizabeth, the sound of her voice caused the unborn John to leap in Elizabeth's womb! Does this suggest that the unborn child was already filled with the Holy Spirit, as mentioned earlier? Whether or not he was, at this point Elizabeth, herself, was filled by the Spirit and exclaimed:

> "Blessed are you among women, and blessed is the fruit of your womb! And why is this granted to me that the mother of my Lord should come to me? For behold, when the sound of your greeting came to my ears, the baby in my womb leaped for joy. And blessed is she who believed that there would be a fulfilment of what was spoken to her from the Lord." (Luke 1:42-45)

Again, we hear of the unborn John leaping in her womb.

The Birth of John the Baptist

We read earlier that Elizabeth did not appear in public for five months. Whether this was five months from the time she conceived or five months from the time she knew she was pregnant, we cannot be sure. However, if the latter then she would still have been confined to the house when Mary arrived and, as mentioned earlier, she was unlikely to have gone far in her last trimester. If this were the case then we can understand that it may not have been until the birth of her baby that "her neighbours and relatives heard that the Lord had shown great mercy to her, and they rejoiced with her" (Luke 1:58).

At that time, the practice was for circumcision to be performed at home, usually by the father. If so, then Zechariah, himself, would have circumcised his son. It was also when the child was given his name, and so we read:

On the eighth day they came to circumcise the child. And they would have called him Zechariah after his father[8], but his mother answered, "No; he shall be called John." (Luke 1:59-60)

This caused some controversy amongst those present, one assumes especially the relatives. Apparently, there was no one in their genealogy, or any relative come to that, who had ever been given the name John. However, it was the father's prerogative to name a child, so the gathered assembly turned to Zechariah. He asked for a writing tablet and wrote, "His name is John", and the gathered assembly were astonished (NIV).

However, as soon as Zechariah wrote those words, having been struck dumb for several months, he began to speak and fear came on all the awe-struck gathering. But more than that:

And all these things were talked about through all the hill country of Judea, and all who heard them laid them up in their hearts, saying, "What then will this child be?" For the hand of the Lord was with him. (Luke 1:65-66)

Zechariah Filled with the Holy Spirit

One of the interesting things to note in the Scriptures is that there is a difference between 'having' the indwelling Holy Spirit and being 'filled' with the Spirit. Frequently we read that when people were 'filled' with the Spirit,[9] they spoke or prophesied about God. However, we must be careful with such words as 'prophesy' or 'prophet'. The role of prophets was to speak on behalf of God, and

---

[8] This was the general Jewish custom: *The Life of Josephus*, 1.
[9] This is dealt with in detail in the *Miracles of the Apostles* by Michael Penny, published by The Open Bible Trust.

although they may have said what God was to do in the future, more often than not they stated what God had done in the past or what He was about to do at that time.

We read that Zechariah was filled with the Holy Spirit and prophesied (Luke 1:67), as his wife Elizabeth had done when Mary first visited her. What he said was in two parts, and concerned two people: the Lord (Luke 1:68-75) and his new-born son John (Luke 1:76-79). What did he say about his son?

> "And you, child, will be called the prophet of the Most High;
>> for you will go before the Lord to prepare his ways,
> to give knowledge of salvation to his people
>> in the forgiveness of their sins,
> because of the tender mercy of our God,
>> whereby the sunrise[10] shall visit us from on high
> to give light to those who sit in darkness and in the shadow of death,
> to guide our feet into the way of peace."

It seems that Zechariah picked up the gist of what Gabriel had told him about John, especially that his son would prepare the way for the Lord. So we see here that Zechariah was speaking about the future, some years ahead, when John would start his ministry. However, as that was about 30 years in the then future, and as Zechariah was already quite old, it is probable that he never saw anything of what he prophesied come to pass.

---

[10] It is possible that Zechariah had in mind Malachi 4:2: "But you who fear my name, the sun of righteousness shall arise with healing in its wings."

The people knew that the Lord's hand was on this child as he grew up (Luke 1:66). The fact that he became strong in the Spirit should not surprise us, as Gabriel said he would be filled with the Holy Spirit from birth. However, at some stage of his life, probably after both his parents had died, possibly when he was around the age of twenty,[11] he went and lived in the desert region[12] and stayed there until the start of his ministry to Israel (Luke 1:80).

---

[11] Norval Geldenhuys, The Gospel of Luke, *The New London Commentary on the New Testament*, page 96.

[12] Probably the region in Judea south of Jericho and west of the Dead Sea.

Chapter 2

The Beginning of John the Baptist's Ministry

Luke is the writer who gives us the precise time when John began his ministry.

> In the fifteenth year of the reign of Tiberius Caesar, Pontius Pilate being governor of Judea, and Herod being tetrarch of Galilee, and his brother Philip tetrarch of the region of Ituraea and Trachonitis, and Lysanias tetrarch of Abilene, during the high priesthood of Annas and Caiaphas, the word of God came to John the son of Zechariah in the wilderness. (Luke 3:1-2)

Both Matthew and Mark, unlike Luke, introduce John without any explanation as to who he was. This may have been because they were writing for a Jewish readership amongst whom, as we shall see, John's fame had spread far and wide. Matthew simply has "In those days John the Baptist came preaching in the wilderness of Judea" (Matthew 3:1), but he says nothing about when 'those' days were. And although Mark has an even briefer statement – he merely says "John appeared" (Mark 1:4) – he does have a preamble about him.

> The beginning of the gospel of Jesus Christ, the Son of God. As it is written in Isaiah the prophet, "Behold, I send my messenger before your face, who will prepare your way, the voice of one crying in the wilderness: 'Prepare the way of

the Lord, make his paths straight,'" John appeared ...
(Mark 1:1-4)

Mark sees the ministry of John as the beginning of the good news concerning Jesus Christ, and as the fulfilment of certain Old Testament prophecies.

- "Behold, I send my messenger before your face, who will prepare your way" is yet another reference back to Malachi (chapter 3 verse 1).
- And "the voice of one crying in the wilderness: 'Prepare the way of the Lord, make his paths straight,'" is from Isaiah 40:3.

And to be fair to Matthew, after having written that John came preaching in the wilderness of Judah, he also linked him with the prophet Isaiah and with the same quotation from Isaiah (see Matthew 3:3).

Luke, also, took the same words from Isaiah but expanded the quotation.

> As it is written in the book of the words of Isaiah the
>   prophet,
> "The voice of one crying in the wilderness:
> 'Prepare the way of the Lord, make his paths straight.
> Every valley shall be filled,
>   and every mountain and hill shall be made low,
> and the crooked shall become straight,
>   and the rough places shall become level ways,
> and all flesh shall see the salvation of God.'"
> (Luke 3:4-6, quoting Isaiah 40:3-5)

The heart of that prophecy [Isaiah 40:3-5] was a metaphor drawn from the ancient custom that when an emperor or some other eminent personage was about to visit a city, the citizens could be required to prepare a well-constructed approach road along which he could advance with due pomp and dignity on his way into the city. Using that metaphor Isaiah predicted that one day Israel would be called upon to prepare an approach road for such a visitor. What visitor? Isaiah left his hearers in no doubt: 'Prepare ... the way for Yahweh ... a highway for our God ... say to the cities of Judah, Behold, your God! Behold, Adonai Yahweh will come as a mighty one.' (David Gooding, *According to Luke*, page 71)

Luke uses these words of the great Messianic prophet Isaiah to describe John's ministry.

Where John Preached

We know that John had been living in the desert region of Judea for some years before the word of the Lord came to him. As mentioned earlier, probably between Jericho and Ein Gedi, west of the Dead Sea. His appearance must have been somewhat different from what the people were accustomed to. Both Matthew and Mark described him as wearing garments of camel hair with a leather belt around his waist, and both say his diet was of one of locusts and wild honey (Matthew 3:4; Mark 1:6).

How long he had lived in the desert region we do not know, but it was in that area where he began his ministry. Matthew 3:1 tells us that it was "in the wilderness of Judea". Luke says it was "all the region around the Jordan" (Luke 3:3). And Mark simply mentions the River Jordan but adds that "all the country of Judea and all Jerusalem were going out to him" (Mark 1:5). Matthew supports this: "Then Jerusalem and all Judea and all the region about the

Jordan were going out to him" (Matthew 3:5). Putting all this together would imply that John was operating in the regions south of Jericho, near where the River Jordan enters the Dead Sea, and not further up north, near the Lake of Galilee, which would have been a very long journey for those in Judea, taking a week or so.

What John Preached

The first words of John, as record by Matthew, were:

> "Repent, for the kingdom of heaven is at hand." (Matthew 3:1-2)

The first word of John's message, like that of Jesus which came a little later (Matthew 4:17), was 'repent', but what did both John, and Jesus, mean by that word? What were they asking the people to do?

'Repentance' means more than a change of mind, more than remorse. From the time of Jeremiah, the [Hebrew] root *sub*, is closely connected with the covenant, and indicates a deliberate turning or returning: the term designates the return of Israel to Yahweh, i.e. to the covenant established between God and his people. 'Repentance' is the radical conversion to God of those who have broken faith with him. (David Hill, *The New Century Bible Commentary; The Gospel of Matthew*, page 90)

Also, to understand what John said, and the force of what he proclaimed, we must have the correct idea as to what he meant, and what those who heard him understood by 'the kingdom of heaven'. This is doubly important as these are also the opening words of Christ's ministry, as recorded in Matthew 4:17.

The 'kingdom of heaven' – the Matthean equivalent for the 'kingdom of God' – means the establishment on earth (not in the heavens) of the sovereign rule and authority of God. (David Hill, *The New Century Bible Commentary, The Gospel of Matthew*, page 90)

This kingdom of heaven is not one which is within people. Such a view is based on a misunderstanding of words recorded in the KJV translation of Luke 17:20-21. There we read:

And when he was demanded of the Pharisees, when the kingdom of God should come, he answered them and said, "The kingdom of God cometh not with observation: neither shall they say, Lo here! or, lo there! for, behold, the kingdom of God is within you."

Clearly no such kingdom could be within the 'you' of the people to whom Christ was speaking; i.e. His enemies, the Pharisees. In most translations we read "the kingdom of God is among you", referring to Himself, the King, being in their midst.

Neither was this kingdom of heaven referring to what Paul wrote about many years later, that the Father "has delivered us from the domain of darkness and transferred us to the kingdom of his beloved Son" (Colossians 1:13).

The people to whom John, and the Lord, were speaking understood their pronouncement to be referring to the kingdom which would originate in heaven but would be upon the earth.[13] It denotes the establishment on earth, not in heaven, of the sovereign rule and authority of God, and this is what Christ told them to pray for:

> "Your kingdom come, your will be done, on earth as it is in heaven." (Matthew 6:10)

And it was this kingdom upon the earth which was the focus of the prophets, especially Isaiah with whom John (and also Jesus) is closely linked. For example:

> It shall come to pass in the latter days
>   that the mountain of the house of the Lord
> shall be established as the highest of the mountains,
>   and shall be lifted up above the hills;
> and all the nations shall flow to it,

---

[13] The 'of' in 'the kingdom of heaven' is the Greek preposition *ton* and is the genitive of origin and takes the meaning 'from'. Thus 'visions of God' are visions 'from' God. So, the kingdom 'of' heaven is the kingdom 'from' heaven. See E W Bullinger, *The Companion Bible* on Matthew 3:2.

and many peoples shall come, and say:
"Come, let us go up to the mountain of the Lord,
    to the house of the God of Jacob,
that he may teach us his ways
    and that we may walk in his paths."
For out of Zion shall go the law,
    and the word of the Lord from Jerusalem.
He shall judge between the nations,
    and shall decide disputes for many peoples;
and they shall beat their swords into ploughshares,
    and their spears into pruning-hooks;
nation shall not lift up sword against nation,
    neither shall they learn war any more. (Isaiah 2:2-4)

"No more shall there be in it
    an infant who lives but a few days,
    or an old man who does not fill out his days,
for the young man shall die a hundred years old,
    and the sinner a hundred years old shall be accursed ...
The wolf and the lamb shall graze together;
    the lion shall eat straw like the ox,
    and dust shall be the serpent's food.
They shall not hurt or destroy
    in all my holy mountain,"
says the Lord. (Isaiah 65:20,25)

This was the kingdom the people of Israel longed for; one without domination by Rome, or any other power, and one where the Messiah would judge the nations from Jerusalem, and peace would reign on earth. This was the kingdom John and Jesus said was 'at hand' and this was the kingdom Christ told them to pray for. It was 'at hand' … but it never came in! Why not?[14]

What John did

It would seem that one necessary condition for the kingdom to come was that the heart of the people of Israel had to be right; so John called for them to repent and offered them baptism as a sign or symbol of repentance.

> In those days John the Baptist came preaching in the wilderness of Judea, "Repent, for the kingdom of heaven is at hand." (Matthew 3:1-2)

> John appeared, baptizing in the wilderness and proclaiming a baptism of repentance for the forgiveness of sins. (Mark 1:4)

> And he went into all the region around the Jordan, proclaiming a baptism of repentance for the forgiveness of sins. (Luke 3:3)

Although various 'washings' were part of the Law of Moses (Leviticus 11-15), the baptism of individual Jews was somewhat new and original, which may be why Mark refers to him as 'John the Baptizer' (RSV, Mark 1:4; 6:14,24; see also footnotes in ESV on Mark 6:14,24). Gentiles who converted to Judaism were baptized[15] (and the men circumcised also), but for an Israelite to be

---

[14] For a more detailed discussion of this question see Appendix 2.

[15] The baptism of Gentiles "washed away the uncleanness from the heathen on entering Judaism, and grafted them with ceremonial purity on to the people of God." (Hans Lietzmann, *Beginnings of the Christian Church*, page 51).

called to undergo this initiation ritual was very different. However, it seems John's ministry initially met with great success.

> And all the country of Judea and all Jerusalem were going out to him and were being baptized by him in the river Jordan, confessing their sins. (Mark 1:5)

> Then Jerusalem and all Judea and all the region about the Jordan were going out to him, and they were baptized by him in the river Jordan, confessing their sins. (Matthew 3:5-6)

In fact, it was so successful that it prompted many of the Pharisees and Sadducees to venture from Jerusalem down to the Jordan[16], wanting to hear what this man was preaching and teaching, but not wanting John to baptize them (Luke 7:30). However, when he saw them coming, he said to them:

> "You brood of vipers! Who warned you to flee from the wrath to come? Bear fruit in keeping with repentance. And do not presume to say to yourselves, 'We have Abraham as our father', for I tell you, God is able from these stones to raise up children for Abraham. Even now the axe is laid to the root of the trees. Every tree therefore that does not bear good fruit is cut down and thrown into the fire." (Matthew 3:7-10)

In his account, Luke does not say that these words were specifically aimed at the Pharisees and Sadducees, but they most likely were. The Pharisees thought that their legalism would give them a

---

[16] The Greek of Matthew 3:7 has coming 'to' the baptism, not coming 'for' the baptism (*Interlinear Greek - Hebrew New Testament*). That is, they came solely to observe.

passport into the kingdom, and the Sadducees their ritual. And both thought that the merits of Abraham were credited to the nation of Israel.

However, if these words were aimed at some of the crowds, they seem to have had the effect John wanted. The crowds wanted to know what they should do to show they had truly repented. "What then shall we do?" they asked, and John answered, "Whoever has two tunics is to share with him who has none, and whoever has food is to do likewise" (Luke 3:10-11).

Even the hated tax collectors[17] came to John and asked "What shall we do?" He told them "Collect no more than you are authorized to do." And there were also soldiers[18] who asked "What shall we do?" and were told "Do not extort money from anyone by threats or by false accusation, and be content with your wages" (Luke 3:12-14).

The result of all of this activity was that "the people were filled with expectation, and all were questioning in their hearts concerning John, whether he might be the Christ" (Luke 3:15). And here, again, we notice the air of expectation which pervaded that society, and which was mentioned a number of times in the Introduction.

And then all three Gospels conclude this episode with more or less the same words. John said to the crowds:

---

[17] Translated 'publicans' in the KJV.
[18] These would not have been Roman soldiers but Jewish ones such as the temple guards, and it would have been some of the temple guards who would have arrested Christ in the Garden of Gethsemane, not Roman soldiers.

"I baptize you with water for repentance, but he who is coming after me is mightier than I, whose sandals I am not worthy to carry. He will baptize you with the Holy Spirit and fire. His winnowing fork is in his hand, and he will clear his threshing floor and gather his wheat into the barn, but the chaff he will burn with unquenchable fire." (Matthew 3:11-12; see also Mark 1:7-8 and Luke 3:16-17)

The wheat, those who repented and bore fruit in keeping with repentance, would be gathered by the One to come. However, the chaff, those who did not repent or feigned repentance, were to be destroyed. And Luke 3:18 states that with many other exhortations John preached good news to the people.

A Very Special Person

We do not know how long John had been preaching and baptising, but eventually Jesus came from Galilee in the north, probably walking down the Jordan valley, to where John was in the south. Matthew gives the fullest account of this episode.

Jesus wanted John to baptize Him but initially John refused (Matthew 3:14). John's baptism was a baptism to symbolise repentance and the forgiveness of sin, but Christ had nothing to repent of and had no sins to be forgiven.[19] John knew this and said to Him "I need to be baptized by you" (Matthew 3:14). John tried to prevent Jesus from being baptized but Christ insisted: "Let it be so now, for thus it is fitting for us to fulfil all righteousness" (Matthew 3:15). What did Christ mean by those words, and why did He want to be publicly baptized?

---

[19] A little later, as we shall see, John called Christ "the Lamb of God, who takes away the sin of the world" (John 1:29) and Peter described him as a lamb "without blemish or spot" (1 Peter 1:19).

The Apostle Paul wrote that:

> For our sake he [God] made him [Jesus] to be sin who knew no sin, so that in him we might become the righteousness of God. (2 Corinthians 5:21)

If this is the case, Jesus had to be publicly identified with sin. He certainly was at the end of His ministry when He was put on the cross, for the Jews considered that anyone who was hung on a tree to die was cursed by God because of their sin (Galatians 3:13). But by undergoing baptism at the start of His ministry Christ not only identified Himself with the human race, He also identified Himself with their sin. And having undergone this public ritual, when He came up from the water, immediately the heavens opened and the Spirit of God descended like a dove and came to rest on Him. Then a voice from heaven said, "This is my beloved Son with whom I am well pleased" (Matthew 3:16-17; see also Mark 1:9-11; Luke 3:21-22).

After His baptism the Lord went into the wilderness for 40 days to be tempted by Satan, and following this experience He was once again seen by John. This episode, and much more, is recorded in the opening chapter of John's Gospel, which also tells us more about John the Baptist.

Chapter 3

The Gospel of John Chapter 1

The opening words of John's Gospel are some of the most loved and well-known in the Bible, and form the last reading in the traditional Christmas carol service. It opens with the words:

> In the beginning was the Word, and the Word was with God, and the Word was God. He was in the beginning with God. All things were made through him, and without him was not any thing made that was made. In him was life, and the life was the light of men. The light shines in the darkness, and the darkness has not overcome it. (John 1:1-5)

This is one of the most Christ-exalting passages in the Scriptures[20], but having given his testimony as to who Jesus is, the writer turns his attention to another person.

John the Baptist Introduced.

> There was a man sent from God, whose name was John. He came as a witness, to bear witness about the light, that all might believe through him. He was not the light, but came to bear witness about the light. (John 1:6-8)

---

[20] Others include Ephesians 1:19b-23; Philippians 2:6-11; Colossians 1:15-20.

Clearly John had a big impact for, as we have seen, huge crowds from Jerusalem and Judea, and from the regions around the Jordan, went to hear him preach and be baptized by him. But we may be wrong to limit his impact to just those who lived permanently in those areas. It is likely that many Jews of the dispersion, visiting Jerusalem, would have made the trip down to the Jordan. For example, Paul, on his first missionary journey, when he spoke in the synagogue in Antioch in Pisidia, referred to John (Acts 13:24-25). And on his third missionary journey, when he arrived in Ephesus, Paul met some Christian Jews (they are called 'disciples') who had been baptized by John (Acts 19:1-4). If the Apostle John wrote his gospel initially for the Jews of the dispersion,[21] one can understand why he included John the Baptist's testimony right at the start. Also, one can begin to appreciate just how much of an influence the Baptist had on the world of Judaism, not only in Jerusalem, Judea and Galilee, but also on those Jews scattered throughout the Roman Empire and beyond.

Returning to Christ, the writer explains that this One who was the Word, who was God, who was there at the beginning of creation, this One "became flesh and dwelt among us, and we have seen his glory, glory as of the only Son from the Father, full of grace and truth" (John 1:14). This is a staggering statement, and to support his testimony as to who Jesus is, the writer points to John the Baptist.

> John bore witness about him, and cried out, "This was he
> of whom I said, 'He who comes after me ranks before me,
> because he was before me.'" (John 1:15)

---

[21] For more on this see *John: His life, death and writings* by Michael Penny, published by The Open Bible Trust.

One needs to ponder just what John said. Jesus, he said, came "*after* me", but He was "*before* me". Seemingly a contradiction, but no! In the flesh Jesus did come after John. He was conceived at least six months after John, and thus born at least six months afterwards. However, He was before John because He was the Word (who became flesh) and as the Word He was there "in the beginning", long before John had been conceived, let alone born.

Questioning John

We now come to a passage which features John being interrogated by priests and Levites from Jerusalem and, apparently, others sent by the Pharisees (John 1:24). The first three questions they asked, with his answers, are as follows.

> They asked: "Who are you?"
> He replied: "I am not the Christ (Messiah)."
> They asked: "What then? Are you Elijah?"
> He replied: "I am not."
> They asked: "Are you the Prophet?"
> He replied: "No."

Although their first question was a simple "Who are you?" clearly John wanted it understood in no uncertain terms that he was not the Christ, their Messiah. In that case, they wanted to know if he was the Messiah's forerunner, Elijah, as per Malachi 3:5. He emphatically denied it. Then they asked him if he was 'the' Prophet? Notice that they did not ask him if he was 'a' prophet, for clearly he was, but who was this 'the' Prophet?

On a number of occasions, the people thought Jesus was 'a' prophet; i.e. just one of the prophets (e.g. Matthew 16:13-14).

However, at other times, some concluded He was 'the' Prophet. For example:

> When the people saw the sign that he had done, they said, "This is indeed *the* Prophet who is to come into the world!" (John 6:14)

> When they heard these words, some of the people said, "This really is *the* Prophet." (John 7:40)

We can easily pass over the use of 'a' and 'the', but we should not. We can, perhaps, gain some understanding of why the use of 'the' Prophet is so different from the use of 'a' prophet, and so much more significant, if we look at Peter's speech to the Jews in Acts 3.

> "Moses said, 'The Lord God will raise up for you a prophet like me from your brothers. You shall listen to him in whatever he tells you. And it shall be that every soul who does not listen to that prophet shall be destroyed from the people.'" (Acts 3:22-23; see Deuteronomy 18:15-19)

Moses was 'the' prophet of the Old Testament. Again, we need to remember that a prophet is a mouthpiece for God who may say what God has done in the past, is doing at that time, or may do in the future. As such Moses was 'the' prophet of the Old Testament. And 'the' Prophet, whom God was to raise up, was the Messiah. Clearly Jesus was 'the' Prophet, the mouthpiece of God, in the New Testament. He was the Messiah.

So, having gained a denial to each of the questions they had posed to John, in frustration, and maybe in desperation with some annoyance in their voice, they said:

"Who are you? We need to give an answer to those who sent us. What do you say about yourself?" (John 1:22)

To which he replied:

"I am the voice of one crying out in the wilderness, 'Make straight the way of the Lord', as the prophet Isaiah said." (John 1:23)

Note: here again John makes another reference to Isaiah. However, their questioning continued:

They asked him, "Then why are you baptizing, if you are neither the Christ, nor Elijah, nor the Prophet?"
John answered them, "I baptize with water, but among you stands one you do not know, even he who comes after me, the strap of whose sandal I am not worthy to untie." (John 1:25-27)

The untying of a sandal was a menial task, performed by a servant of low status or slaves with no rights. This is how John saw himself when compared to Christ. What his listeners made of that answer, we do not know. Whether or not it satisfied them, whether or not they understood what John had said or to whom he was referring, is doubtful as Jesus had just recently come onto the scene. However, as far as the writer of the gospel was concerned, that was the end of that interview, but, he does tell us that:

These things took place in Bethany across the Jordan, where John was baptizing. (John 1:28)

Now there is some confusion as to where 'Bethany across the Jordan' is located, as there seemed to have been no such place by that name in that area. Some place it just north of the Dead Sea, east of Jericho (see first map below), but others place it further north, just south of the Sea of Galilee, possibly at Tishbe, near the Brook Cherith (see second map below), which was where Elijah was fed by ravens (1 Kings 17:2-4).

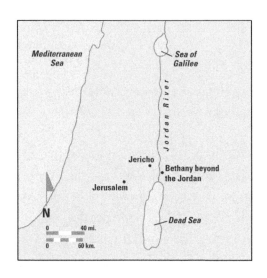

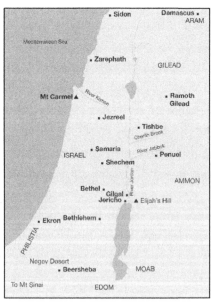

As mentioned earlier, many who visited John came from Jerusalem and Judea (as did the priests and Levites and those who were sent by the Pharisees to interview John). For those to travel all the way to Galilee and back would have taken many days; nearly a week there and a week back. And also, John 3:23 tells us that later John did go further north, up as far as Aenon (see page 48). So, I find the suggestion that Bethany was east of Jericho, as indicated on the first map above, more credible.

Also, John Marsh, in his commentary *Saint John* (page 123), states there is textual evidence that the name should be *Bethabara*, which was a town on the east side of the Jordan (see map below).

John's Testimony about Jesus

John the Baptist's testimony concerning Christ included five statements about Him.

The gospel states that it occurred the day after the priests and Levites had questioned him, and clearly it took place sometime after he had baptized the Lord and seen the Spirit descend upon Him (see John 1:32). The first thing we read is:

> The next day he [John the Baptist] saw Jesus coming towards him, and said, "Behold, the Lamb of God, who takes away the sin of the world! This is he of whom I said, 'After me comes a man who ranks before me, because he was before me.' I myself did not know him, but for this purpose I came baptizing with water, that he might be revealed to Israel." (John 1:29-30)

First, one wonders to whom John was speaking? One assumes the priests and Levites had returned to Jerusalem so it may have been to some of his disciples or to some of the people who had come to him to be baptized. His testimony first of all stated:

> That Jesus was the Lamb of God, who takes away the sin of the world.

And then,

> That Jesus was the One who ranked before John because He was before John. (Compare this with John 1:15 and the earlier comments on that verse.)

John then added two further important pieces of information about Jesus.

> First, John bore witness that he had seen "the Spirit descend from heaven like a dove" and that the Spirit remained on Christ.

And then he added that God, who had sent him to baptize with water, had told him that, "He on whom you see the Spirit descend and remain, this is he who baptizes with the Holy Spirit" (John 1:32-33).

John's fifth and final point, perhaps the climax of his testimony, was:

> "And I have seen and have borne witness that this is the Son of God." (John 1:34)

As John the Baptist had had such a big impact on the people of Israel, both those living in the land and those outside, one can see why the gospel writer included this powerful testimony. The purpose of the Gospel was to prove that "Jesus is the Christ (Messiah), the Son of God" (John 20:30-31). Including this powerful testimony of John the Baptist right at the beginning would have made the Jewish readers at that time sit up and listen.

However, it is strange to read that John said "I myself did not know him" (John 1:33). They were related, and maybe when they were children they would have met. But John had been living in the desert region south of Jericho for many years before he started his ministry, during which time Jesus was living in Nazareth in Galilee, in the north. Not only that, when Jesus came to John to be baptized it seems John did recognise him. We read:

> Then Jesus came from Galilee to the Jordan to John, to be baptized by him. John would have prevented him, saying, "I need to be baptized by you, and do you come to me?" (Matthew 3:14)

The problem seems to lie with the word "know". The Greek word is *oida* and W E Vine[22] states it means 'to know him perfectly', and E W Bullinger[23] says of this word that it can have the meaning of 'perceive'. Thus, when Jesus came to John to be baptized, John was acquainted with Him and recognised Him and knew much about Him, that He was different and special. However, John did not perceive, know fully, just who Jesus was; he did not know Him perfectly. This fuller knowledge came only when he saw the dove descend and rest on Jesus, and when he heard the voice from heaven say, "This is my beloved Son, with whom I am well pleased" (Matthew 3:16-17). John then knew that this Jesus was the Messiah.

John's Disciples

John's testimony concerning Jesus bore early fruit. We read that the next day John was standing with two of his disciples and Jesus walked by. He looked at Jesus and said to the two disciples, "Behold, the Lamb of God!" and they followed Jesus and stayed with Him for the rest of that day. One of the two was Andrew, Simon Peter's brother, who straightaway went and found his brother Simon and said to him, "We have found the Messiah" and he brought him to Jesus (John 1:35-42).

Not only did John's testimony bear early fruit, it bore fruit of the highest quality; Andrew and Simon Peter.

---

[22] *Expository Dictionary of New Testament Words.*
[23] *A Critical Lexicon and Concordance.*

Chapter 4

John the Baptist and his Disciples

John Moves North

Time marches on, and following the wedding in Cana in Galilee and Jesus' meeting with Nicodemus, we read that:

> After this Jesus and his disciples went into the Judean countryside, and he remained there with them and was baptizing. John also was baptizing at Aenon near Salim, because water was plentiful there, and people were coming and being baptized (for John had not yet been put in prison). (John 3:22-24)

Now from both Mathew's Gospel and Mark's, we could get the impression that John was imprisoned immediately after Christ's temptations (Matthew 4:12; Mark 1:14), but this was clearly not the case. Even before the Lord's temptation Luke wrote about John being imprisoned. However, he does not state that it was at that time that Herod Antipas had arrested him. He wrote that it was after John had rebuked Herod, an event which took place a little while after the Lord's temptations (Luke 3:19-20). And in John's Gospel, as we have seen, John was still active for quite a while, during a number of Christ's visits and activities in other places.

We, in the 21st century, living in industrialised, westernised societies, are dominated by time. We like information in chronological order, and want to know how long it is between events. However, that is not the case in all societies today, and certainly was not so in ancient cultures, including the world of Jews in the 1st century. I will attempt to present the life of John the Baptist in chronological order, in as near a time order as I am able, but if the reader disagree in places, that is perfectly understandable.

Following His cleansing of the temple and His discussion with Nicodemus, which also, one presumes, took place in Jerusalem, Jesus and His disciples left the city and went into the Judean countryside. However, John had moved from the region just north of the Dead Sea further up the Jordan to Aenon, on the opposite side of the Jordan to Tishbe and Brook Cherith. The reason for doing so was that there was more water there. By the time the River Jordan reached the region of the Dead Sea it could be quite low, especially in the dry season. This would also have had the advantage that his ministry would have been more accessible to the people of Galilee.

More Testimony from John

We are told first that some of John's disciples got into a discussion with a particular Jew over purification (John 3:25). This was a big issue in Judaism but we are given none of the details.

However, John's disciples were rather concerned about him, as the size of his following was decreasing. They came to John and said, referring to Jesus, "Rabbi, he who was with you across the Jordan, to whom you bore witness—look, he[24] is baptizing, and all are going to him" (John 3:26). John was not the least bit perturbed by people leaving his band and going to follow Jesus. In fact, he rejoiced. John answered his disciples' concern with these words:

> "A person cannot receive even one thing unless it is given him from heaven. You yourselves bear me witness, that I said, 'I am not the Christ, but I have been sent before him.' The one who has the bride is the bridegroom. The friend of the bridegroom, who stands and hears him, rejoices greatly at the bridegroom's voice. Therefore this joy of mine is now complete. He must increase, but I must decrease." (John 3:27-30)

So John saw the number of his disciples as given him by God, and he was content with whatever following he had, but he rejoiced greatly over the fact that more and more were following Jesus. After all, said John, "I am not the Christ". He saw himself, again, as the one who went before Him to prepare the way. And he uses a lovely picture, taken from a wedding ceremony. He depicts Christ as the groom, and himself as the best man, the one who stands beside the groom and the one who rejoices at what the groom has

---

[24] John 4:2 tells us that Jesus was *not* baptising people, but His disciples were.

to say. No doubt John had heard Jesus preach and teach on a number of occasions, and what he heard the Saviour say had caused him to rejoice so much so that he said that his joy was now complete. And he closed with one of his familiar and important themes: Christ must increase and he must decrease.

Did John say this?

However, am I right in saying that these words 'closed' what John the Baptist was saying? Some translations have the following verses, 31 to 36, surrounded by inverted commas (e.g. the NASB, NKJV, earlier editions of the NIV), taking the position that these words were uttered by John. However, others (e.g. the ESV, NRSV, ASV, REB, the latest edition of the NIV) do not have the inverted commas and see these words as put in by the writer of the Gospel. They are certainly Christ exalting words and worthy to be read. Whether they came from the mouth of John or the pen of the writer, is, perhaps, a secondary issue.

> He who comes from above is above all. He who is of the earth belongs to the earth and speaks in an earthly way. He who comes from heaven is above all. He bears witness to what he has seen and heard, yet no one receives his testimony. Whoever receives his testimony sets his seal to this, that God is true. For he whom God has sent utters the words of God, for he gives the Spirit without measure. The Father loves the Son and has given all things into his hand. Whoever believes in the Son has eternal life; whoever does not obey the Son shall not see life, but the wrath of God remains on him. (John 3:31-36)

In John 1:10-11 we read:

He was in the world, and the world was made through him, yet the world did not know him. He came to his own, and his own people did not receive him.

This was clearly written after the people of Israel had rejected Him and crucified Him. And similarly, we read in John 3:32 that "no one receives his testimony". This does not fit in with the positive, optimistic and rejoicing words of John in 3:27-30 and, again, is more in line with being written after the crucifixion.

Jesus goes North

They say 'News travels fast' and not only had John's disciples noticed the declining support for John and the growing support for Jesus, others also had.

> Now when Jesus learned that the Pharisees had heard that Jesus was making and baptizing more disciples than John (although Jesus himself did not baptize, but only his disciples), he left Judea and departed again for Galilee. (John 4:1-3)

Why He did this, we are not told, but perhaps there were already murmurings against Jesus and threats to His life. However, it seems that when He was in Galilee an issue arose about fasting and prayers, which concerned John's disciples and many others. The three Synoptic Gospels all record that this episode took place in Galilee.

- Matthew 9:1 has Him arriving by boat to His own town, generally accepted to be Capernaum on the north shore.
- Mark 2:1 states clearly that it was in Capernaum.

- Luke 5:1 has Jesus standing by Lake Gennesaret, which was another name for the Sea of Galilee.

However, there are slight differences as to who asked the question.

- Matthew 9:14 has "the disciples of John came to him, saying ..."
- Mark 2:18 has "the people came and said to him ..."
- Luke 5:33 simply has "they said to him ...". However, if we look back a couple of verses it seems the 'they' may well have included Pharisees and teachers of the law.

Prayer and fasting were big issues in that society. The Pharisees fasted twice a week (Luke 18:12) and encouraged their disciples to do likewise. However, Christ warned against making the practice a sign of spirituality (Matthew 6:16-18). Similarly, they loved to offer lengthy prayers in public places and Christ, again, warned against this (Matthew 6:5-7) and the prayer He gave as an example was quite short (Matthew 6:9-13; see also Luke 18:11-14). As fasting was such a big issue one can well-understand why different groups came and asked Him very similar questions.

- Then the disciples of John came to him, saying, "Why do we and the Pharisees fast but your disciples do not fast?" (Matthew 9:14)
- Now John's disciples and the Pharisees were fasting. And people came and said to him, "Why do John's disciples and the disciples of the Pharisees fast, but your disciples do not fast?" (Mark 2:18)
- And they said to him, "The disciples of John fast often and offer prayers, and so do the disciples of the Pharisees, but yours eat and drink." (Luke 5:33)

In His reply the Lord totally ignores the issue of praying. He focuses solely on fasting[25] and, in His answer, He uses the same figure that John had used, that of a wedding where He is the bridegroom.

> "Can the wedding guests mourn as long as the bridegroom is with them? The days will come when the bridegroom is taken away from them, and then they will fast." (Matthew 9:15; see also Mark 2:19-20 and Luke 5:34-35)

As people often fasted after a death, or at other times of mourning, one can understand why the Lord used the figure of a bridegroom at a marriage and said what He did. It would be as inappropriate for His disciples to fast then, as it would be for the wedding guests to fast at a wedding, which was a time for rejoicing.

---

[25] In the Law of Moses, the Jews were ordered to fast on just one day a year, the Day of Atonement (Leviticus,16:29) where 'afflict yourselves' or 'deny yourselves' (NIV) refer to fasting. However, as time went by some practised fasting at times of disaster (Nehemiah 1:4), and others as a sign of mourning (2 Samuel 1:12) or repentance (1 Kings 21:27). During the Babylonian exile fasting became an increasingly outward ritual with little spiritual value which is why the prophets spoke against it (Zechariah 7:5). However, even though not sanctioned by God the practice continued to grow and by New Testament times it had become a fixed practice with the Pharisees and many of their followers fasting regularly twice a week, with much outward show (Luke 18:12; Matthew 6:16; 9:14).

Chapter 5

John the Baptist in Prison

Very early in his Gospel, soon after he introduced John and wrote about his ministry, and even before Luke wrote about the baptism of Jesus, Luke inserted a few words about John and Herod Antipas.

> So with many other exhortations he [John] preached good news to the people. But Herod the tetrarch, who had been reproved by him for Herodias, his brother's wife, and for all the evil things that Herod had done, added this to them all, that he locked up John in prison. (Luke 3:18-20)

Clearly this incident occurred much later, as its position half-way through Matthew's Gospel would suggest.

> For Herod had seized John and bound him and put him in prison for the sake of Herodias, his brother Philip's wife, because John had been saying to him, "It is not lawful for you to have her." And though he wanted to put him to death, he feared the people, because they held him to be a prophet. (Matthew 14:3-5)

Mark adds some further details.

> For it was Herod who had sent and seized John and bound him in prison for the sake of Herodias, his brother Philip's wife, because he had married her. For John had been saying

to Herod, "It is not lawful for you to have your brother's wife." And Herodias had a grudge against him and wanted to put him to death. But she could not, for Herod feared John, knowing that he was a righteous and holy man, and he kept him safe. When he heard him, he was greatly perplexed, and yet he heard him gladly. (Mark 6:17-20)

From this account it would appear that by putting John in prison Herod was, in some way, protecting him. And it looks as if John may have been in prison for quite some while, for it seems Herod, not infrequently, would see John and listen to him ... gladly! However, one thing that annoyed Herod, and his wife, was John kept saying their marriage broke the Law of Moses, which it did.

If a man takes his brother's wife, it is impurity. He has uncovered his brother's nakedness; they shall be childless. (Leviticus 20:21; see also 18:16)

The Herods were never popular, or fully accepted by the Jews. Herod the Great's rise to power was largely due to his father's good standing with Julius Caesar, who entrusted him with the public affairs of Judea. Then, in about 40 BC, the Senate in Rome made Herod 'King of the Jews'. However, the Herods were not Jews, they were from Idumea, but the Scriptures stated that the king not only had to be a Jew, but also had to be a descendant of David.

When Herod the Great died he divided his kingdom between three of his sons: one of them was Herod Antipas, the one who imprisoned John, and he had been granted Galilee and Peraea. However, Antipas, like all the Herods and their families, posed as conforming Jews, adhering to the Law of Moses, so Antipas could rightly be criticised by John.

Initially he was married to the daughter of Aretas, the ruler of the Nabateans, and after he had divorced her to marry Herodias, the Nabateans made war against Herod Antipas, who called on Rome for help and support.

As we have seen John operated primarily in the Jordan Valley, the east side of which was under Herod Antipas' jurisdiction, so one can appreciate that he was a constant thorn in the flesh. According to Josephus, John was imprisoned in Herod's combined fortress, palace and prison of Machaerus, on the east side of the Dead Sea (see map below, and *Antiquities of the Jews* 18,5,2).

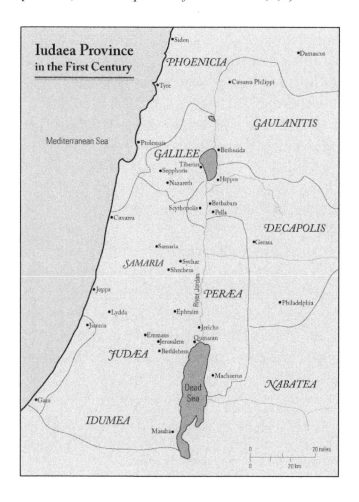

John doubts Jesus

Earlier, John's followers were decreasing in numbers and Jesus's were increasing, and John rejoiced. However, John was now in prison, and may have been there for some time, but Jesus was out and about, teaching and preaching in the cities, towns and villages. News of Him spread throughout the whole of Judea and the surrounding countryside, even down to Machaerus, in southern Perea, where John was in prison. However, he still had some disciples and they also kept him informed about "the deeds of Jesus" (Matthew 11:2).

So Jesus was free, and John was in prison, with the threat of death hanging over him. Things were not working out as John had expected. He had preached "Repent, for the kingdom of heaven is *at hand*", but there were no visible signs, that he could see, that this kingdom on the earth was being set up. He called two of his disciples and sent them to Jesus to ask:

> "Are you the one who is to come, or shall we look for another?" (Matthew 11:3; Luke 7:19)

But one wonders, how could John doubt?[26] He was full of the Holy Spirit, and had been so since birth. He had baptized Jesus, seen the heavens open, seen the dove descend and land on Jesus, and heard the voice from heaven say "This is my beloved Son in whom I am well pleased". One might suspect that John doubting would have disappointed the Lord but, as we shall see, after He had answered

---

[26] Whereas I am inclined to the view that the question John asks suggests that John had doubts as to whether or not Jesus was the Messiah, there is another view which is explained in Appendix 1.

their question and sent them back to John, the Lord praised the Baptist and lifted him above all men.

However, the Lord did not give John's disciples a straight answer. In front of their very eyes, He performed many miracles of healing (Luke 7:21) and then turned to them and said:

> "Go and tell John what you have seen and heard: the blind receive their sight, the lame walk, lepers are cleansed, and the deaf hear, the dead are raised up, the poor have good news preached to them. And blessed is the one who is not offended by me." (Matthew 11:4-6; Luke 7:22-23)

The miracles which Jesus performed were not solely acts of mighty power, they were 'signs' which signified that He was the Christ/Messiah and the Son of God (John 20:30-31). What John's disciples saw was what the prophet Isaiah said would happen when the Messiah would come to save them.

> Say to those who have an anxious heart,
>   "Be strong; fear not!
> Behold, your God
>   will come with vengeance,
> with the recompense of God.
>   He will come and save you."
> Then the eyes of the blind shall be opened,
>   and the ears of the deaf unstopped;
> then shall the lame man leap like a deer,
>   and the tongue of the mute sing for joy.
> (Isaiah 35:4-6)

Clearly, at that point in time, John had an anxious heart. However, as a man who knew the Scriptures and what his disciples had seen, what Jesus told them to say, would have been a far more affirmative answer than a simple 'Yes!' And Christ added to the prophecy of Isaiah by saying an even greater miraculous sign was being performed, "the dead are raised up".

Christ's final comments to John's disciples were "Blessed is the one who is not offended by me." The word 'blessed' here is the Greek *makarious*, which means to be happy or content; i.e. words of encouragement, to ease John's anxieties.

Jesus praises John

It would seem that there were many people around when John's disciples came to Jesus, to ask if He was the One. This may have caused some in the crowd to doubt or question John, or lower John in their estimation, but Christ would have none of it. He spoke to the crowd about John, first of all making them think, by asking them quite ironic questions.

> "What did you go out into the wilderness to see?
>> A reed shaken by the wind?
> What then did you go out to see?
>> A man dressed in soft clothing?
>> Behold, those who wear soft clothing are in kings' houses.
> What then did you go out to see?
>> A prophet?
>> Yes, I tell you, and more than a prophet."
> (Matthew 11:7-9; Luke 7:24-26)

Clearly many of these people had gone out in the wilderness to see John, but they did not see a reed which bent with the wind. Rather they saw a man who preached repentance and who held rigidly and unwaveringly to the Law of Moses, which was why Herod Antipas had imprisoned him.

But what did they see? A man in fine linen? No! A man dressed in camel skins with a leather belt.

Did they see a prophet? Yes! They all believed that John was a prophet, and Herod Antipas knew this also, for although he wanted to put John to death, he feared the people, because they held him to be a prophet (Matthew 14:3-5).

But Christ said that he was "more than a prophet". In what way was he "more than a prophet"? Christ continued:

> "I tell you, and more than a prophet. This is he of whom it is written,
>> 'Behold, I send my messenger before your face,
>> who will prepare your way before you.'
> Truly, I say to you, among those born of women there has arisen no one greater than John the Baptist." (Matthew 11:9b-11a; Luke 7:26b-28a)

Here we see Christ applying the prophecy of Malachi 3:1 to John.

> "Behold, I send my messenger, and he will prepare the way before me. And the Lord whom you seek will suddenly come to his temple; and the messenger of the covenant in whom you delight, behold, he is coming, says the LORD of hosts." (Malachi 3:1)

John was the 'messenger', but the "messenger of the covenant", used later in the verse, is used in the Old Testament of the Messiah; e.g. see later in Malachi 3. So the Lord designates John as that special messenger who was to precede the Messiah. And then He exalted John to a position higher than any other human being that has ever lived. Great praise indeed ... especially for a man who had his doubts.

Jesus Addresses the Crowd

However, the Lord then turned to the people with words of great encouragement and promise for them.

> "Yet the one who is least[27] in the kingdom of heaven is greater than he." (Matthew 11:11b; Luke 7:28b)

All too often people look for wealth on this earth and greatness in the eyes of other people. Many believers in Christ may not look for those things, but they often feel that their faith is weak and their works are poor. However, even the one with the least faith in Christ will be greater in eternity than John the Baptist was on earth. These words of Christ are worthy of much meditation.

The crowd to whom Jesus spoke seems to have been made up of two groups: those who had been baptized by John and those who had not. Following His statement about the kingdom of heaven, we read:

> When all the people heard this, and the tax collectors too, they declared God just, having been baptized with the baptism of John, but the Pharisees and the lawyers rejected

---

[27] The Greek word here is *mikroteros* and E W Bullinger, in a note on this verse in *The Companion Bible,* states "lease = less: i.e. younger, meaning Himself". In other words, the Lord, who was younger than John the Baptist, would be greater than him in the kingdom.

the purpose of God for themselves, not having been baptized by him. (Luke 7:29-30)

It would seem that those who acknowledged they were sinners and who had repented and been baptized by John, and held him to be a prophet (such as the tax collectors, Luke 3:12-13), concluded that what Christ said about John showed that God was just. However, those who had gone to John satisfied with their own righteousness, and who questioned him, refused to repent and declined to be baptized (such as the Pharisees and lawyers; Matthew 3:7-8) ... these had basically rejected God's purpose.

The next verse is rather difficult to understand in the ESV.

> "From the days of John the Baptist until now the kingdom of heaven has suffered violence, and the violent take it by force." (Matthew 11:12; see also Luke 16:16)

However, the earlier editions of the NIV have:

> "From the days of John the Baptist until now, the kingdom of heaven has been forcefully advancing, and forceful men lay hold of it."

If this second translation is nearer to the Greek one can understand that forceful, strong men, like John the Baptist, had advanced and attracted other strong characters, like some of John's disciples, such as Andrew, who went and followed Jesus. However, most modern translations (e.g. the NKJV, as well as the later versions of the NIV) seem to favour the former translation. If that be the case, what did Christ mean, if, indeed, Christ uttered those words? One suggestion is that these words are a comment by Matthew about the persecution the Christian Jews had been suffering up to the time he wrote.

> It sounds much more like a comment of Matthew than a saying of Jesus. It sounds as if Matthew was saying: "From the days of John, who was thrown into prison, right down to our own times the Kingdom of Heaven has suffered violence and persecution at the hands of violent men." (William Barclay, *The Daily Study Bible, The Gospel of Matthew*)

This was certainly the case, because following John's imprisonment, and subsequent death, opposition to Christ grew, resulting in His crucifixion. Then, when we enter the Acts Period, violence at the hands of the Jewish leadership, grew against the Apostles and other Jewish Christians.

David Hill[28] takes a similar line, suggesting that the "now", in Matthew 11:12, may refer to the time when Matthew wrote his Gospel.

Whether or not the words of Matthew 11:12 are Christ's, or an interpolation by Matthew, we may not know, but the next statements did come from the lips of the Saviour.

> "For all the Prophets and the Law prophesied until John, and if you are willing to accept it, he is Elijah who is to come. He who has ears to hear, let him hear." (Matthew 11:13-15)

---

[28] *The New Century Bible Commentary, The Gospel of Matthew.*

Here Christ seems to be saying that John was the last in the line of Old Testament prophets. There were certainly many who had the gift of prophecy following the Pentecost of Acts 2, but those who possessed it were not prophets in the mould of the Old Testament prophets and certainly did not have their authority and standing.

The expression "He who has ears to hear, let him hear" usually follows a difficult saying, and that is the case here. Having declared that John was definitely the messenger of Malachi 3:1 (see Matthew 11:10 and Luke 7:27), the Lord does not, however, totally endorse John as fulfilling the Elijah prophecy of Malachi 4:5. This is one of a number of ambiguous statements concerning whether or not John was Elijah, and these are all dealt with in Appendix 3.

This Generation

The expression "this generation" is found frequently in the Gospels but often refers to those who refused to accept Jesus. That being the case, it would seem that the following words were aimed at the Pharisees and lawyers. They had rejected God's purposes by first being satisfied with their own righteousness and then by failing to respond to John's call for repentance and baptism, and now were growing stronger and stronger in their opposition to Jesus.

> "To what then shall I compare the people of this generation, and what are they like? They are like children sitting in the market-place and calling to one another,
> > 'We played the flute for you, and you did not dance;
> > we sang a dirge, and you did not weep.'
> For John the Baptist has come eating no bread and drinking no wine, and you say, 'He has a demon.' The Son of Man has come eating and drinking, and you say, 'Look at him! A glutton and a drunkard, a friend of tax collectors and

sinners!' Yet wisdom is justified by all her children." (Luke 7:31-35; see also Matthew 11:16-19)

Christ likened those who opposed Him and John to children playing in the market place, and who could not agree on which game to play and which was the best game: weddings or funerals.[29] John and Jesus were two very different characters who presented the same message – "Repent, for the kingdom of heaven is at hand" – in two very different ways.

John came from the desert region of Judea and was an only child. He lived a solitary life, and dressed in camel skins and a leather belt. He ate locust and honey, and drank no alcohol. He ministered along the Jordan valley.

Jesus came from Galilee, from a large family. He wore ordinary clothes, and ate and drank normal food with a variety of people. He ministered throughout the towns and cities of Galilee and Judea.

Yet we can imagine the criticisms of the Pharisees and those who opposed. John was odd; he dressed oddly; he ate strange food; he did not enjoy the ordinary pleasures of life; clearly, he had a demon! But of Jesus they could say that He likes to eat and drink wine, He mixes with everyone and anyone, even the tax collectors and sinners. John's ascetic lifestyle was insane, and Christ was lax and careless about the people He mixed with.

Maybe the parallels were, John sang a dirge, but they were not moved. Christ played a flute, but they did not rejoice. They were like children who would not join in, no matter what the game. They were determined to sit on the side-lines and pick fault.

---

[29] Christ may have had Ecclesiastes 3:4 in mind: "a time to weep, and a time to laugh; a time to mourn, and a time to dance".

But Christ's final words to them were:

> "Yet wisdom is justified (shown to be right) by all her children."

The ultimate verdict on the teaching of both Jesus and John lay with its effect on the people who heard it, not with those who criticized it. The Pharisees and company may have argued against John and ignored his pleas for repentance and refused to be baptized. To justify such action, they may have disparaged John, but he had moved men's hearts towards God as they had not been moved for hundreds of years, since the days of Malachi or earlier. He had got them to repent and be baptized.

They may well have criticised Christ as the friend of sinners and ignored His call to repent, but He had brought new life to people, one of love and forgiveness, and He had held out to them eternal life.

Thousands had followed John and his message, and even more ultimately followed Christ and His teaching. The wisdom of Jesus and John was shown to be right by the many who responded.

Chapter 6

The Death of John the Baptist

It seems that John was in prison for some time as we read that Herod liked to talk with him and heard him gladly (Mark 6:20). However, Herod did not want to execute John because he feared the people, who considered John to be a prophet (Matthew 14:5).

Understandably, when we know what John was saying about her, Herod's wife, Herodias, held a grudge against him, and wanted to kill him. However, she could not give that command, and Herod would not do so for, as we have just noted, Herod feared the people. Also he seemed to respect John, knowing that he was a righteous and holy man, and so he protected him, and he did like to speak with John even though he was probably often puzzled and perplexed by what John said (Mark 6:19-20).

As mentioned, we do not know how long John was in prison, but on the occasion of Herod Antipas' birthday, things were to change. He organised a banquet for his officials and military commanders, including the leaders of Galilee – remember that Herod Antipas ruled over Galilee and Perea. His step-daughter[30] came into the hall and danced. It is a safe assumption that at such gathering the dance would have been of a suggestive nature and generally performed by a slave girl. Hence some have questioned whether a Herodian

---

[30] Not named in the Bible but Josephus names her as Salome; *Antiquities of the Jews* 18,5,4.

princess would dance before such a gathering. However, A E J Rawlinson maintains that Salome's dance …

> … is not wholly incredible, however outrageous, to those who know anything of the morals of oriental courts, and of Herod's family in particular. (*The Gospel According to Saint Mark,* page 82)

Her dance seemed to have pleased all the guests and stirred Herod's emotions so much that he rashly promised her whatever she wished. He repeated that promise and swore on oath "Ask me for whatever you wish, and I will give it to you … up to half my kingdom" (Mark 6:22-23).

She went and consulted with her mother, Herodias, concerning what she should ask for. Back came the answer – the head of John! The young girl rushed back to the king and announced "I want you to give me at once the head of John the Baptist on a platter" (Matthew 14:8; Mark 6:25).

This must have seriously surprised Antipas, who was greatly distressed, but what could he do? He had made a public promise on oath in front of his guests. He could not lose face, so he gave the command.

> Immediately the king sent a soldier of the guard with orders to bring John's head. He went and beheaded him in the prison, brought his head on a platter, and gave it to the girl. Then the girl gave it to her mother. (Mark 6:27-28)

When John's disciples heard about it, they took his body, and laid it in a tomb (Mark 6:29), and Matthew adds that they then went and told Jesus (Matthew 14:12). And this must have distressed the Lord greatly for when He heard about it, He took a boat and sailed alone to a solitary place (Matthew 14:13).

Josephus' Account

It is interesting to read what Josephus has to say on the death of John.

> Now some of the Jews thought that the destruction of Herod's army came from God, and that very justly, as a punishment of what he did against John, that was called the Baptist: for Herod slew him, who was a good man, and commanded the Jews to exercise virtue, both as to righteousness towards one another, and piety towards God, and so to come to baptism; for that the washing [with water] would be acceptable to him, if they made use of it, not in order to the putting away [or the remission] of some sins [only], but for the purification of the body; supposing still that the soul was thoroughly purified beforehand by righteousness. Now when [many] others came in crowds about him, for they were very greatly moved [or pleased] by hearing his words, Herod, who feared lest the great influence John had over the people might put it into his power and inclination to raise a rebellion, [for they seemed ready to do any thing he should advise,] thought it best, by putting him to death, to prevent any mischief he might cause, and not bring himself into difficulties, by sparing a man who might make him repent of it when it would be too late. Accordingly he was sent a prisoner, out of Herod's suspicious temper, to Macherus, the castle I before mentioned, and was there put to death. Now the Jews had an opinion that the destruction of this army was sent as a

punishment upon Herod, and a mark of God's displeasure to him. (*Antiquities of the Jews,* 18, 5, 2)

We have already mentioned the war between Herod and Aretas, the ruler of the Nabateans, following Herod divorcing his daughter.

John Raised from the Dead?

After a period of isolation following the death of John, Jesus resumed His ministry. Crowds followed Him on foot from town to town, and He healed the sick. Herod Antipas heard about all of the miracles that Jesus was doing and concluded that John had been raised from the dead and that was why Jesus had the power to heal, and why He could work miracles (Matthew 14:1-2). Why did Herod come to such a conclusion? From where did he get such an idea?

By this time Jesus had appointed the Twelve and they, too, were teaching and healing. People everywhere were talking about this amazing situation, and coming to different conclusions about its leader, Jesus.

> Some were saying, "John the baptizer has been raised from the dead; and for this reason these powers are at work in him." But others said, "It is Elijah." And others said, "It is a prophet, like one of the prophets of old." (Mark 6:14-15)

But of all the suggestions, which would Herod accept?

> But when Herod heard of it, he said, "John, whom I beheaded, has been raised." (Mark 6:16)

Pangs of conscience may have caused Herod to initially accept this explanation, for as we have already seen "Herod feared John, knowing that he was a righteous and holy man, and he kept him safe" (Mark 6:20). However, Luke states that in the end Herod seems to have come to a more rational conclusion.

> Herod said, "John I beheaded; but who is this about whom I hear such things?" And he tried to see him [Jesus]. (Luke 9:9)

Whether Herod ever did see Jesus soon after this, we do not know, as there is no mention in the New Testament of him doing so. However, he did meet Jesus in Jerusalem after Jesus' arrest. When Pilate learnt that Jesus was from Galilee he sent Him to Herod, as Galilee came under his jurisdiction. We read that Herod was delighted to see Jesus, and asked many questions, but the Lord remained silent, and did not answer him (Luke 23:5-9).

Confusion about Jesus and John

It is clear that following John's execution there arose confusion as to whether or not Jesus was John raised from the dead, and this continued for a little while. And people were talking so much about Jesus and making all sorts of suggestions as to who He was. One time, when He was near Caesarea Philippi, between the Lake of Galilee and Damascus, He asked His disciples, "Who do people say that the Son of Man is?" (Matthew 16:13). Their answer was:

- Some say John the Baptist,
- but others Elijah,
- and still others Jeremiah
- or one of the prophets.

It is interesting to stop and consider each of these opinions.

John the Baptist

It may seem strange to us that any should think the Lord Jesus to be John the Baptist, but they were related, through Mary and Elizabeth. Origen[31] suggests there may have been some physical, family resemblance. However, what they taught, and some of what they did, was the same. For example:

1. Both opened their ministry with the words "Repent, for the kingdom of heaven is near." (Matthew 3:2; 4:17)
2. Both were associated with baptism. (John 1:25-27; 3:22-23; 4:1-2)
3. Both upheld the Law of Moses. (Matthew 14:2-4; 5:17-19)

However, it still seems strange that people thought Jesus to be John. By this time John had been dead for a little while, but it seems that Herod, himself, may have fuelled the view that Jesus was John, and people often follow the views of their leaders. As we have seen, at one time Herod did say that Jesus was John the Baptist raised from the dead, which was why, in Herod's mind, Jesus had such miraculous powers (Matthew 14:1-2).

---

[31] "Origen points out that Mary, the Mother of Jesus, and Elizabeth, the mother of John, were closely related (Luke 1:36). That is to say, Jesus and John were blood relations. And Origen speaks of a tradition which says that Jesus and John closely resembled each other in appearance." See William Barclay, *The Daily Study Bible, The Gospel of Matthew.*

Elijah

The view that the Lord Jesus was Elijah is not the least bit strange. It is very understandable. As we have mentioned the last prophet sent to Israel was Malachi, and his words close the Old Testament.

> "Behold, I will send you Elijah the prophet before the great and awesome day of the LORD comes. And he will turn the hearts of fathers to their children and the hearts of children to their fathers, lest I come and strike the land with a decree of utter destruction." (Malachi 4:5-6)

The last statement from God to the people of Israel in Old Testament times was that Elijah was to come before the great and dreadful day of the Lord. And as the years of Daniel's seventy sevens were ticking by, it is not surprising that some Jews thought John the Baptist to be Elijah (John 1:20-25), and neither is it surprising that some thought the Lord Jesus to be Elijah. Even today, at some of their religious celebrations, some Jews place an empty chair at the table in case Elijah comes.

Jeremiah

As well as having their Scriptures, our Old Testament, the Jews of Christ's day also had what many call the *Apocrypha*. They also possessed various other non-canonical books such as *The Assumption of Moses* and *The Book of Enoch* which are alluded to in the letter of Jude. At least two books in the *Apocrypha* refer to Jeremiah.

2 Maccabees 2:1-12 states that before the Babylonian Exile, Jeremiah took the tent, the Ark of the Covenant and the altar of incense out of the Temple and hid them in a cave in Mount Nebo.

2 Esdras 2:18 states, "I will send you help, my servants Isaiah and Jeremiah". Some Jews believed that before the coming of the Messiah, Jeremiah would return, recover the ark and the altar of incense, and the glory of God would once more come upon the people of Israel.

In stating that Jesus was Elijah or Jeremiah, the people of that day were giving Him high honour, for Elijah and Jeremiah were the expected forerunners, and when they arrived, the Messiah and the kingdom would shortly follow.

One of the Prophets

This answer is also understandable. John the Baptist was looked upon by the people as a prophet from God, and Christ gave him that status also (Matthew 11:9-13; 14:5). Jesus applied the word to Himself and the people saw Him as "the prophet from Nazareth in Galilee" (Matthew 13:57; 21:11). People could see that what He was doing was different, and that this made Him different (note Nicodemus' words in John 3:2).

However, seeing Jesus as 'a' prophet, as 'one' of the prophets, is an incomplete truth. He was more than 'a' prophet; He was 'the' prophet like Moses. Moses was the major prophet spoken of in the Old Testament, and Jesus is 'the' prophet of the New Testament and He fulfilled a major prophecy given to Moses in Deuteronomy 18:15-19:

> The Lord your God will raise up for you a prophet like me from among your own brothers. You must listen to him. For this is what you asked of the Lord your God at Horeb on the day of the assembly when you said, "Let us not hear the

voice of the Lord our God nor see this great fire anymore, or we will die."

The Lord said to me: "What they say is good. I will raise up for them a prophet like you from among their brothers; I will put my words in his mouth, and he will tell them everything I command him. If anyone does not listen to my words that the prophet speaks in my name, I myself will call him to account.

Peter spoke of this in Acts 3:22-23:

"For Moses said, 'The Lord your God will raise up for you a prophet like me from among your own people; you must listen to everything he tells you. Anyone who does not listen to him will be completely cut off from among his people.'"

The Christ, the Son of God

Having heard the disciples tell Him who others thought He was, Jesus then asked them directly "But who do you say that I am?" and Peter replied, "You are the Christ, the Son of the living God." Jesus answered him: "Blessed are you, Simon Bar-Jonah! For flesh and blood has not revealed this to you, but my Father who is in heaven" (Matthew 16:15-17).

Shorter versions of this episode can be read in Mark 8:27-29 and Luke 9:18-20.

Chapter 7

Further References to John the Baptist in the Gospels

In John's Gospel

There are two other passages in John's Gospel which refer to John the Baptist.

We read in John 5:18 that the Jews were trying to kill Jesus, not only because He was breaking their interpretation of the Sabbath Laws, but also, and more importantly, He was calling God His own Father, and so making Himself equal with God. In His argument with them, He twice referred to John.

> "There is another who bears witness about me, and I know that the testimony that he bears about me is true. You sent to John, and he has borne witness to the truth. Not that the testimony that I receive is from man, but I say these things so that you may be saved. He was a burning and shining lamp, and you were willing to rejoice for a while in his light.
>
> But the testimony that I have is greater than that of John. For the works that the Father has given me to accomplish, the very works that I am doing, bear witness about me that the Father has sent me." (John 5:32-36)

To quell their opposition, He appealed first of all to John's testimony, again showing how popular and influential John had been. And John had borne witness to the fact that Jesus was the Christ. In effect, Christ was saying, "If you won't listen to what I say about myself, listen to what John said about me, and if you do and believe, you may be saved."

But then He appealed to a greater witness, the works that He was doing. The miracles, the miraculous *signs*, signified that He was the Christ/Messiah, the Son of God (John 20:30-31). Amongst the many kinds of miraculous signs He was doing, Jesus was performing the ones that the prophet Isaiah said the Saviour would do (Isaiah 35:4-6).

Later in John's Gospel we read of another encounter Christ had with the opposition and again He appealed to the miraculous works that He was doing.

> "If I am not doing the works of my Father, then do not believe me; but if I do them, even though you do not believe me, believe the works, that you may know and understand that the Father is in me and I am in the Father." (John 10:37-38)

Following this we read that the authorities again tried to arrest Him, but He escaped and went away across the Jordan, to the place where John had been baptizing at first, and there He remained for a while. When there, many came to Him and said, "John did no [miraculous] sign, but everything that John said about this man was true." And as a result of what John had said, many there believed in Him (John 10:39-42). And so John's influence continued after his death.

After the Transfiguration

The Transfiguration is an episode in Christ's life which has caused much confusion in the minds of some Christians. How did His glory shine through? How was Moses raised from the dead and afterwards, did he go back to the grave? And what about Elijah? Where did he come from and where did he go? However, all these questions are irrelevant if we just notice from the text that this was not a real event but a vision[32] (Matthew 17:9). Neither Elijah nor Moses was there in person.

After Peter, James and John had seen the vision and were coming down the mountain, the Lord turned to them and commanded them not to tell anyone about the vision until after He had been raised from the dead. In response to this, the disciples asked what may appear to be rather an unrelated question, namely "Then why do the scribes say that first Elijah must come?" (Matthew 17:10). However, this is not such an unrelated question. Malachi recorded that:

> "Behold, I will send you Elijah the prophet before the great and awesome day of the Lord comes. And he will turn the hearts of fathers to their children and the hearts of children to their fathers, lest I come and strike the land with a decree of utter destruction." (Malachi 4:5-6)

So the day of the Lord was to precede the coming of the Messiah, and this is what the scribes correctly taught. So, if Christ was the Messiah and He was to die and rise from the dead then … what about Elijah? Wasn't he to come first? Christ answered them

---

[32] The ESV, KJV and others correctly translate the Greek word *horama* as 'vision', as in Acts 9:10,1; 11:5 and elsewhere

"Elijah does come, and he will restore all things. But I tell you that Elijah has already come, and they did not recognize him, but did to him whatever they pleased. So also the Son of Man will certainly suffer at their hands." Then the disciples understood that he was speaking to them of John the Baptist. (Matthew 17:11-13)

Many find these verses confusing, and they are. Look at the tenses.

- Elijah does come, and will restore all things – future.
- Elijah has already come – past tense.

The disciples understood that the Lord was speaking about John the Baptist, but John did not restore all things! He suffered and was executed, and so, too, would the Lord Jesus.

This is another one of those ambiguous statements, similar to the earlier one in Matthew 11:13-15, concerning whether John was or was not Elijah, and this one, and the others, are dealt with in Appendix 2.

The Transfiguration is also described in Mark 9:2-13 and Luke 9:28-36. Mark's account also contains the disciples' question about Elijah coming first, but the narrative does not mention John the Baptist by name, and Luke contains neither their question nor Christ's answer.

John's Baptism: From God or from man?

Following His triumphal entry into Jerusalem, on what has become known as Palm Sunday, Christ had a hectic few days. He healed people, and drove from the temple those who sold and bought in its courts, and He overturned the tables of the money-changers. He had many arguments with the authorities and on one of the days, as He was walking in the temple, the chief priests and the scribes and the elders challenged Him: "By what authority are you doing these things, or who gave you this authority to do them?" His reply was:

> "I will ask you one question; answer me, and I will tell you by what authority I do these things. Was the baptism of John from heaven or from man? Answer me." (Mark 11:29-30)

This put them on the spot, but it was not a trick question. The correct answer to His question would automatically lead to them knowing the answer to their question.

> The right answer to His question would also answer theirs … John the Baptist had borne testimony to Jesus as the Messiah. If they acknowledged him to be a prophet with divine authority, the answer to their question was plain, and they would see that the authority of Jesus was derived from the same source. (C E Graham Swift, *The New Bible Commentary Revised*, page 876)

So these leaders gathered together and reasoned … "If we say, 'From heaven', he will say, 'Why then did you not believe him?' But if we say, 'From man'?" … but they could not say that out loud, publicly, for they were afraid of the people who held that John really was a prophet. So, they answered Jesus, "We do not know." As a result, Jesus said to them, "Neither will I tell you by what authority I do these things" (Mark 11:31-33).

Chapter 8

John the Baptist in the Acts of the Apostles

Two Baptisms

Almost the last statement our Lord made to His disciples before He ascended into heaven referred to John the Baptist.

> And while staying with them he ordered them not to depart from Jerusalem, but to wait for the promise of the Father, which, he said, "you heard from me; for John baptized with water, but you will be baptized with the Holy Spirit not many days from now." (Acts 1:4-5)

This takes us back to the very beginning of John's ministry when he said to the crowds, including Pharisees and Sadducees:

> "I baptize you with water for repentance, but he who is coming after me is mightier than I, whose sandals I am not worthy to carry. He will baptize you with the Holy Spirit and fire. His winnowing fork is in his hand, and he will clear his threshing floor and gather his wheat into the barn, but the chaff he will burn with unquenchable fire." (Matthew 3:11-12; see also Mark 1:7-8 and Luke 3:16-17)

And about ten days after Christ said those words and ascended into heaven, they were baptized by the Holy Spirit who came upon them, not in the form of a dove, but as tongues of fire.

The importance of John's Baptism of Jesus

Following Judas' betrayal of Christ and his subsequent suicide, it was 'necessary' to make the number of Apostles back up to Twelve. Christ had told them:

> "Truly, I say to you, in the new world, when the Son of Man will sit on his glorious throne, you who have followed me will also sit on twelve thrones, judging the twelve tribes of Israel." (Matthew 19:28; see also Luke 22:30)

Peter raised this issue with the 120 who were gathered in the upper room in the days between the Lord's Ascension and the coming of the Spirit and stated that it was 'necessary' (Acts 1:21, NIV) to do this. But who could fill this gap? It could not be just anyone. Peter explained the condition:

> "So one of the men who have accompanied us during all the time that the Lord Jesus went in and out among us, beginning from the baptism of John until the day when he was taken up from us—one of these men must become with us a witness to his resurrection." (Acts 1:21-22)

There were two who met this criterion – Joseph and Matthias – and we need to stop and consider the implication of what Peter said. There are three issues.

1) Why was it necessary for Judas' replacement to have witnessed John's baptism of Jesus? It was on that occasion when the heavens opened and the Holy Spirit, in the form of a dove, descended and landed on Him and remained there for some time. And also, there was the voice from heaven which said, "This is my beloved Son in whom I am

well pleased." These two saw and heard all of this and so could give a personal testimony as eye-witnesses of this event.

2) However, if it was necessary for these two to have witnessed this, what about the other eleven? Were they present also? Andrew most probably was, as he was one of John's disciples (John 1:35-40). So, were Peter, James and John and the others amongst the crowd on that very special day?

3) Also, if it was necessary for Judas' replacement to have accompanied Jesus and the Twelve all[33] the time that the Lord was ministering, does that mean that Christ was often accompanied by more than Twelve men most of the time? Art and films often depict him with just the Twelve, but that seems not to have been the situation. And this would also be the case with the Last Supper. Joseph and Matthias would have been there and so, too, one suspects, was the unnamed disciple who took Peter into the courtyard of the high priest (John 18:15-16), and the young man of Mark 14:51-52.

Peter and Cornelius

It was not until Acts 10 that the Lord directed Peter to preach to a Gentile, the God-fearing[34] Roman Centurion, Cornelius. It would

---

[33] We must always be careful with universal words like 'all' and 'everyone' as they seldom take their literal meaning. For example, at the start of the meeting we may ask "Is everyone here?" and we understand that to mean everyone of a certain group. And we know during Christ's time on earth He sometimes took just Peter, James and John with Him.

[34] Proselytes were Gentiles who had converted to Judaism and needed to have been circumcised and keep the Sabbath (see, for example, Isaiah

seem that Cornelius had been stationed in the area for some time and Peter pays him the compliment of knowing what had happened many years earlier.

> "As for the word that he [God] sent to Israel, preaching good news of peace through Jesus Christ (he is Lord of all), you yourselves know what happened throughout all Judea, beginning from Galilee after the baptism that John proclaimed: how God anointed Jesus of Nazareth with the Holy Spirit and with power." (Acts 10:36-38)

Peter started his narrative by referring to John's baptism and the anointing of Jesus with the Holy Spirit when the Lord went to John to be baptized. This, seemingly, Cornelius was aware of.

It is, perhaps, not surprising that he had heard of John for we read that crowds and crowds followed him. Also, when Herod beheaded John, this was against Roman Law. It seems Rome did nothing about it, but no doubt it was talked about in Roman ranks.

Peter in Jerusalem

When Peter returned from his visit to Cornelius, he was criticised by some of the Jewish Christians in Jerusalem: "You went to uncircumcised men and ate with them" (Acts 11:3). Peter gave a

---

56:6-7). These could enter the inner parts of the temple and the central body of the synagogues. God-fearers were Gentiles who believed in the God of Israel, but who had not been circumcised and in the synagogues had to sit separately, and they could only enter the outer courts of the temple. Many were very devout, such as Cornelius (see Acts 10:1-2) and the Centurion who built the synagogue in Capernaum (Luke 7:1-6). And there were many such God-fearers in the synagogues of the Dispersion which Paul visited on his missionary journeys, a number of which became Christians.

full explanation, starting with the vision he had received and the Spirit telling him to go to Cornelius. He concluded with a reference to John's baptism.

> "As I began to speak, the Holy Spirit fell on them just as on us at the beginning. And I remembered the word of the Lord, how he said, 'John baptized with water, but you will be baptized with the Holy Spirit.' If then God gave the same gift to them as he gave to us when we believed in the Lord Jesus Christ, who was I that I could stand in God's way?" (Acts 11:15-17)

This, again, shows how important and influential John and his ministry was years after his death. What Peter said convinced his opposition, for they glorified God and said "Then to the Gentiles also God has granted repentance that leads to life" (Acts 11:18).

Paul in Antioch in Pisidia

One may wonder what Paul peached in the many synagogues that he visited. He was 'A Missionary of Genius' and modified how he presented his message depending on whom he was addressing.[35] We can see this by comparing what he said to:

- The pagans in the market place in Lystra (Acts 14:15-17);
- The philosophers on Mars Hill (the Areopagus) in Athens (Acts 17:22-31);
- The Jews and God-fearing Gentiles in the synagogue at Antioch in Pisidia (Acts 13:16-41).

---

[35] For more on this see *Paul: A Missionary of Genius* by Michael Penny and *The Speeches in Acts* by W M Henry, both published by The Open Bible Trust.

The speech in this synagogue is by far and away the longest we have recorded, and is packed with references to the Old Testament Scriptures. It is probably typical of what he preached to Jewish audiences wherever he went. He started by giving a brief synopsis of the history of Israel up to David and then said:

> "Of this man's [David's] offspring God has brought to Israel a Saviour, Jesus, as he promised. Before his coming, John had proclaimed a baptism of repentance to all the people of Israel. And as John was finishing his course, he said, 'What do you suppose that I am? I am not he. No, but behold, after me one is coming, the sandals of whose feet I am not worthy to untie.'" (Acts 13:23-25)

Paul then went on to talk about the message of salvation, but why did he bring in John the Baptist? After all Paul had never met him and Antioch was some 900 miles from the Jordan Valley! As mentioned earlier, it may well be that John's influence went far wider than the Jordan Valley and Judea, reaching many Jewish societies of the dispersion. When they visited Jerusalem for one of the major feast days, a number may well have gone down to the Jordan to see and hear this man that everyone was talking about, and then they talked about John when they returned home. Some probably repented and were baptized by John, and what a story that would be.

Paul in Ephesus

I have just suggested that John's influence was extensive, reaching not only those Jews in Jerusalem, Judea and Galilee, but also the Jews of the Dispersion who lived in many parts of the Roman world, and beyond. We have seen Paul refer to John in the synagogue in Antioch, and next we have an example in Ephesus, even further away from Jerusalem and the Jordan, some 1,100 miles.

On his third missionary journey Paul paid a second visit to the city of Ephesus. There he found some disciples, some Christian Jews, and he asked them whether or not they had received the Holy Spirit: this may seem an unusual question to us today, but I will return to it shortly (Acts 19:1-2). They replied that they had not even heard of the Holy Spirit, which is rather surprising as the Spirit is mentioned in the Old Testament. Paul then enquired as to their baptism, and they informed him they had been baptized by John (Acts 19:3), to which Paul replied:

> "John baptized with the baptism of repentance, telling the people to believe in the one who was to come after him, that is, Jesus." (Acts 19:4)

As soon as they were told this Paul baptized them in the name of the Lord Jesus and when he laid his hands on them, the Holy Spirit came on them (Acts 19:5-6). So, again, we can see just how far and wide John's influence was.

Now, there are some seemingly unusual things going on here. To understand these, we need to realize that during the period of time covered by the Acts of the Apostles, God was dealing with the Gentiles differently from the way He dealt with the Jews. For example, as soon as Gentiles believed they received the Holy Spirit. There was no need for them to be baptized or to have hands laid on them (see, for example Cornelius and company in Acts 10:43-47).

However, for the Jews, and those related to the Jews like the Samaritans (who could trace their ancestry back to Abraham via

Isaac), not only did they have to believe in Jesus, they needed to be baptized in His name and also to have the hands of an Apostle, or a senior Jewish Christian, laid on them. Only then did the Holy Spirit come upon them.[36] For example:

> Now when the apostles at Jerusalem heard that Samaria had received the word of God, they sent to them Peter and John, who came down and prayed for them that they might receive the Holy Spirit, for he had not yet fallen on any of them, but they had only been baptized in the name of the Lord Jesus. Then they laid their hands on them and they received the Holy Spirit. (Acts 8:14-17)

This was also the case for Paul himself.

> So Ananias departed and entered the house. And laying his hands on him he said, "Brother Saul, the Lord Jesus who appeared to you on the road by which you came has sent me so that you may regain your sight and be filled with the Holy Spirit." And immediately something like scales fell from his eyes, and he regained his sight. Then he rose and was baptized. (Acts 9:17-18)

And, as we have seen, this was also the case with those Jewish disciples in Ephesus.

The reason for this may have been to establish the Apostles as God's new leaders. The kings were not even Jews and the priesthood was corrupt. The curtain which separated the Holy Place from the Most Holy Place (which only the high priest could enter)

---

[36] For more details on this see *The Miracles of the Apostles* by Michael Penny, published by The Open Bible Trust.

was torn in two, showing that the high priest had lost his privileged position.

In Conclusion

The reference, in Acts 19:4, is the last reference to John the Baptist in the Bible. Ephesus is some 1,800 km (over 1,100 miles) from the Jordan Valley over land, and the events described in Acts 19 took place some 30 years after John had been beheaded. These two facts alone show just how influential he had been. His own description of himself was "the voice of one crying out in the wilderness, 'Make straight the way of the Lord.'" He certainly did that, and did so very effectively.

Chapter 9

A Tribute to John the Baptist

What can we say about this unique human being, the only one who has ever been filled with the Holy Spirit from before birth? Yet when he commenced his ministry the Spirit led him not to Jerusalem and the cities, but into the Jordan valley, not to the green banks of the Jordan near the Sea of Galilee, rather to the more desolate and desert-like region just north of the Dead Sea.

He did not go to the people; the people came to him. They flocked to him in their thousands. So great was his impact that the Jewish leaders, the Scribes and Pharisees and Sadducees, left the comfort of Jerusalem to travel to the wilderness region where he was preaching. He was the last in the line of those Old Testament prophets and, just as those earlier prophets had done, John castigated the leaders.

Although he never left the Jordan valley, both he and his message went far and wide. Paul, nearly twenty years later, referred to him in his speech in the synagogue in Antioch in Pisidia, 900 miles away. And several years later, on his third missionary journey, Paul met believers in Ephesus, a further 200 miles away, who had been baptized by John.

It is doubtful if Pontius Pilate based in Caesarea, as far west from the Jordan as you can get in Israel, bothered much about this man, dressed in camel skins held together by a leather belt. However, the king, Herod Antipas, felt the force of the Baptist's tongue, so stinging that he had him imprisoned and ultimately put to death.

If he had had a grave stone or a tomb, I wonder what would have been inscribed. Perhaps the most fitting epitaph for him are those words of our Lord Jesus Christ:

> "among those born of women
> there is no one greater than John"
> (Luke 7:28)

Appendix 1: John the Baptizer. A Doubter?

By Roy Ginn

Whereas many have suggested that when John the Baptizer sent his disciples to Jesus to ask "Are You the Coming One or do we look for another?" (Luke 7:19) that he had begun to have doubts as to whether or not Jesus was the Messiah. However, I believe that there is an alternative view.[37]

Luke 7:18-23 and Matthew 11:2-5, record the event under consideration. In Luke 7:19, John says "Are You the Coming One, or do we look for another?" (NKJV). John had previously referred to the Lord as the *Lamb of God* (John 1:29 & 36), and as the *Son of God* (John 1:34). The Lord Himself generally used the title *Son of Man*; so why then did John select the title "The Coming One" on this particular occasion? This title comes from the Old Testament, and I believe John selected it deliberately, as a *Remez*.

The first century Rabbis used a technique that was called *Remez* (hint). In their teaching, they would use part of a Scripture passage in a discussion which hinted at another part that preceded or followed it. All Jewish children were expected to learn, off by heart, the Books of Moses, by the time they had reached the age of twelve. So, in the course of time, as their understanding grew, they

---

[37] This article was first published in *Search* magazine, Number 221, December 2020.

would be able to get the hint, and thus understand the point being made. There were no printed scriptures in those days. They had to study the scrolls in the synagogues. The Lord, being a Rabbi, used this method Himself. [38]

We may use such a method today. If someone were to call me a name, I may respond by saying "sticks and stones!" Why would I say that? If you knew the rhyme you would get the message! I was hinting at the last part, "names will never hurt me".

I believe John was referring to Zechariah 9:9-11, the last phrase being "I will set your prisoners free from the waterless pit". John was in prison when he spoke those words. I believe that John was asking if the Lord was going to come and release him from prison so that he could continue his work, or had his work come to an end? The Lord's reply was taken from more than one place in Isaiah, but with notable words omitted:

> 35:5-10. The "Ransomed" are the released prisoners (v 10)
> 42:6-7.   Release of prisoners (v 7)
> 61:1.   Opening the prison

The Lord, using the Remez, left out the parts about release from prison. This would be important in itself, but when you realise that Herod was a suspicious man and had his spies everywhere, you see how important it was not to ask the question directly. The Lord knew what John was really asking because he understood John's methodology, and He answered with the same technique.

---

[38] For more on this see "The second encounter", page 14, of *Nicodemus: Understanding 'Being born again'* by Roy Ginn, published by The Open Bible Trust.

Also, in Matthew 11:6, and Luke 7:23, the Lord says "blessed is he who is not offended in Me". How could anything the Lord had said or done be offensive to John? – it is what he was expecting to see. I think the Lord was basically saying that John's work was now over, and that he had earned the "well done thou good and faithful servant". He just had to hang on in there.

Appendix 2:
The Kingdom of Heaven
is at hand

John the Baptist opened his ministry with the words:

> "Repent, for the kingdom of heaven is at hand." (Matthew 3:2)

And our Lord Jesus Christ began His ministry with the same words: see Mathew 4:17. However, that kingdom of heaven never arrived, yet it was 'at hand', 'near' (KJV). What happened? Some have reinterpreted this kingdom to be a 'spiritual' kingdom, or say such things as it refers to believers so that when people are saved they 'join the kingdom'. However, we have stated earlier that it denotes the establishment on earth, not in heaven, of the sovereign rule and authority of God, and this is what Christ told them to pray for: "Your kingdom come, your will be done, on earth as it is in heaven" (Matthew 6:10). That being the case, we need to answer the question, why did this kingdom of heaven on earth not happen?

Conditional Prophecies

Some people have the view that every action is pre-ordained or pre-determined by God. However, He is not like that. Consider the following statement from the Lord.

> "If at any time I declare concerning a nation or a kingdom, that I will pluck up and break down and destroy it, and if that nation, concerning which I have spoken, turns from its

evil, I will relent of the disaster that I intended to do to it. And if at any time I declare concerning a nation or a kingdom that I will build and plant it, and if it does evil in my sight, not listening to my voice, then I will relent of the good that I had intended to do to it." (Jeremiah 18:7-10)[39]

We can see this in a number of places in the Old Testament when He did not follow through on a judgement He had announced, quite simply because people repented: the classic one being Nineveh at the less than enthusiastic preaching of Jonah.

Sometimes a nation was given an option. For example, consider Israel. They were told by the Lord:

> "If you are willing and obedient, you shall eat the good of the land; but if you refuse and rebel, you shall be eaten by the sword; for the mouth of the Lord has spoken." (Isaiah 1:19-20)

This was in harmony with Deuteronomy 28, an important chapter in understanding the Lord's dealings with Israel throughout the Scriptures.[40] It states that if they obeyed the Law and commandments, certain blessings would follow. However, if they did not, judgments would be the consequence. Following Isaiah's prophecy, Israel initially repented and obeyed the Law, but later strayed from the Law and fell into idolatry. As a result, they were conquered by a foreign nation, the Babylonians: all in harmony with Deuteronomy 28:49-50.

---

[39] For more on this see *A Key to Unfulfilled Prophecy: Jeremiah 18:7-10* by Michael Penny, published by The Open Bible Trust.
[40] For more on this see *Deuteronomy 28: A Key to Understanding* by Michael Penny, published by The Open Bible Trust.

In the opening words of both the ministries of our Lord and John the Baptist, there were two important, linked parts: "Repent" ... for the kingdom of heaven is ... "at hand". If the people repented, the kingdom of heaven, which was at hand, would come in. If they did not repent, it would not. Initially things looked good, with thousands flocking to John, to repent and be baptized. Christ, at first had similar success but He could see inside people and He told some that they only followed Him because of the miracles and later many turned back and no longer followed Him (John 6:2,66).

The crowds in Jerusalem waved palm branches and shouted "Hosanna". However, a few days the cry from the centre of that city was "Crucify him. Crucify him!". Was that kingdom from heaven still "at hand"?

Restoring the Kingdom to Israel

On the cross the Lord Jesus prayed, "Father, forgive them, for they know not what they do" (Luke 23:34). That prayer was not for the Roman soldiers but primarily for the people of Israel (Acts 2:23; 3:15; 5:30). Our Lord's prayer was answered and so not all was lost, and after 40 days of the resurrected Christ teaching His disciples, they asked Him.

> "Lord, will you at this time restore the kingdom to Israel?"
> (Acts 1:6)

And He replied:

> "It is not for you to know times or seasons that the Father has fixed by his own authority." (Acts 1:7)

In other words, He was not going to tell them because it depended upon … What? Whether or not the people of Israel repented, and this is exactly what Peter urged them to do.

> "Repent therefore, and turn again, that your sins may be blotted out, that times of refreshing may come from the presence of the Lord, and that he may send the Christ appointed for you, Jesus, whom heaven must receive until the time for restoring all the things about which God spoke by the mouth of his holy prophets long ago." (Acts 3:19-21)

So if the nation repented, not only would their sins be blotted out, but also God would send back Christ who would restore all things, including the kingdom.

Initially the response was good, with 3,000 rising to 5,000, repenting and being baptized (Acts 2:41; 4:4). However, it wasn't long before opposition raised its ugly head and all except the Apostles fled from Jerusalem (Acts 8:1). And when we read of persecution in the New Testament, it is not the persecution of Nero, which did not start until after the period of time covered by the Acts of the Apostles had ended. New Testament persecution is of Jewish Christians by the Jewish authorities.

This opposition and persecution came to a head some 25 years later, about the time Paul arrived in Rome. We read from Josephus that the high priest Ananus had James, the brother of Jesus, and others stoned to death in Jerusalem.

> But this younger Ananus, who, as we have told you already, took the high priesthood, was a bold man in his temper, and very insolent; he was also of the sect of the Sadducees, who

are very rigid in judging offenders, above all the rest of the Jews, as we have already observed; when, therefore, Ananus was of this disposition, he thought he had now a proper opportunity [to exercise his authority]. Festus was now dead, and Albinus was but upon the road; so he assembled the sanhedrin of judges, and brought before them the brother of Jesus, who was called Christ, whose name was James, and some others, [or, some of his companions]; and when he had formed an accusation against them as breakers of the law, he delivered them to be stoned. (Josephus, *Antiquities of the Jews*; 20,89,1)

This seemed to have been the last straw, for Paul announced that "God's salvation has been sent to the Gentiles" and added "and they will listen" (Acts 28:28). Earlier he had pronounced Isaiah's judgmental prophecy upon the people of Israel (Acts 28:26-27; quoting Isaiah 6:9-10) and within about seven years of that judgmental statement, the Romans destroyed Jerusalem and the temple. They killed thousands of Jews and took those remaining as slaves and scattered them throughout the Roman Empire, another example of Deuteronomy 28:49-50.

The Jews, and especially the Jewish leadership, did not repent at the call of John or the preaching of Jesus or the urging of Peter and the Twelve, and so the kingdom from heaven, which had been "at hand" no longer was. The offer, so to speak, had been withdrawn.

Appendix 3:
John the Baptist
and Elijah

Introduction

Why did some of the Jewish leaders ask John the Baptist if he was Elijah? And why did some think that Jesus may have been Elijah? (See John 1:21; Matthew 16:14.) And why are there nearly 30 references to Elijah in the Gospels?

Elijah was the beginning of a long line of prophets that the Lord sent to the People of Israel. He was not the first prophet, for that distinction belongs to Moses (Deuteronomy 18:15), or possibly Enoch (Jude 14). Elijah was followed by Elisha and eventually by Isaiah, Jeremiah and company, ending with Malachi, the last of the Old Testament prophets. However, Malachi was not the last prophet, for that distinction belongs to John the Baptist (Luke 16:16, see also Matthew 11:13). Even though others after John had the gift of prophecy and were called prophets, they were not of the same order. Elijah and John, however, are more inter-linked than just being the first and last of that line of 'prophets'. What do we know of these two men? How do their lives intertwine?

Elijah

Elijah came onto the scene during the reign of King Ahab (1 Kings 17). When challenged as to his authority, credibility and suitability for the office of prophet, he was authenticated by having the power to perform miracles, which his successor, Elisha, also had.

However, this ability ceased with successive prophets. This was also the case with Moses and the Law, with the Judges, and also with the Apostles. In all these cases there was an initial surge of miracles which later waned.

If people are asked about Elijah, what most know about him was his departure from this earth, not by death and burial, but by a chariot of fire.

> Then Elijah took his cloak and rolled it up and struck the water, and the water was parted to one side and to the other, till the two of them could go over on dry ground.
>   When they had crossed, Elijah said to Elisha, "Ask what I shall do for you, before I am taken from you." And Elisha said, "Please let there be a double portion of your spirit on me." And he said, "You have asked a hard thing; yet, if you see me as I am being taken from you, it shall be so for you, but if you do not see me, it shall not be so." And as they still went on and talked, behold, chariots of fire and horses of fire separated the two of them. And Elijah went up by a whirlwind into heaven. And Elisha saw it and he cried, "My father, my father! The chariots of Israel and its horsemen!" And he saw him no more. Then he took hold of his own clothes and tore them in two pieces. (2 Kings 2:8-12)

But if that is the most memorable thing the Old Testament says of Elijah, the least memorable, particularly with Gentile Christians of today, are the closing verses of the Old Testament.

> "Behold, I will send you Elijah the prophet before the great and awesome day of the Lord comes. And he will turn the hearts of fathers to their children and the hearts of children

to their fathers, lest I come and strike the land with a decree of utter destruction." (Malachi 4:5-6)

This sending of Elijah, this return of Elijah, this second coming of the prophet, as mentioned above, is probably one of the least known and most frequently ignored teachings concerning Elijah, at least in Gentile Christian circles. However, this is *not* the case in Jewish circles where, at each Passover Feast, they leave a chair empty in case Elijah should return.

"But they are wrong!" Gentile Christians protest. "John the Baptist was Elijah. He fulfilled those prophecies!" But did he? That is a very interesting question and one worthy of careful consideration.

John the Baptist

Luke opens his gospel, not with the birth of our Lord Jesus, but with the sad plight of a childless couple: the priest Zechariah and his wife Elizabeth, who was barren. They were both well on in years, possibly past the age of child bearing for the woman. One day it was Zechariah's turn to burn incense in the temple. When there, the Angel Gabriel appeared to him.

> And Zechariah was troubled when he saw him, and fear fell upon him. But the angel said to him, "Do not be afraid, Zechariah, for your prayer has been heard, and your wife Elizabeth will bear you a son, and you shall call his name John. And you will have joy and gladness, and many will rejoice at his birth, for he will be great before the Lord. And he must not drink wine or strong drink, and he will be filled with the Holy Spirit, even from his mother's womb. And he will turn many of the children of Israel to the Lord their God, and he will go before him in the spirit and power of

Elijah, to turn the hearts of the fathers to the children, and the disobedient to the wisdom of the just, to make ready for the Lord a people prepared." (Luke 1:12-17)

He will go before the Lord, in the spirit and power of Elijah! So ... was John the Baptist to be Elijah? Gabriel doesn't seem to say so, but what did John think? What was his answer, for this very question was put to him early in his ministry?

As we know John's message was "Repent, for the kingdom of heaven is at hand" (Matthew 3:2) and as a sign of their repentance, individual Jews came to John to be baptized. He must have had an exceptional effect upon the Israel of his day. That nation had had no word from the Lord, no prophet, for 400 years. After such a period of silence, the quiet was broken in the Desert of Judea, down by the River Jordan. A man clothed in camel's hair, with a leather belt,[41] called people to repent and be baptized. But he called those who came forward but did not want to repent and be baptized "A brood of vipers!" Such words were addressed to the Pharisees and Sadducees, but the Jewish leadership could not dismiss him. Who was this person who preached so powerfully, who baptized true repentants, and who verbally abused the hypocrites? They wanted to know more.

> And this is the testimony of John, when the Jews sent priests and Levites from Jerusalem to ask him, "Who are you?" He confessed, and did not deny, but confessed, "I am not the Christ." And they asked him, "What then? Are you Elijah?" He said, "I am not." "Are you the Prophet?" And he answered, "No." So they said to him, "Who are you? We need to give an answer to those who sent us. What do you

---

[41] Just like Elijah, 2 Kings 1:8.

say about yourself?" He said, "I am the voice of one crying out in the wilderness, 'Make straight the way of the Lord', as the prophet Isaiah said." (John 1:19-23)

So, was John the Baptist Elijah? He, himself, said he wasn't and his only description of himself is based on neither Malachi 3:1 nor Malachi 4:5, but upon Isaiah 40:3: "I am the voice of one calling in the wilderness, 'Make straight the way for the Lord.'"

So that must settle the issue then! If John said he wasn't Elijah, then he could not have been Elijah! True? Well there is a far higher authority than John who does not give such an unequivocal answer – our Lord Jesus Christ! What did He have to say on this matter?

> As they went away, Jesus began to speak to the crowds concerning John: "What did you go out into the wilderness to see? A reed shaken by the wind? What then did you go out to see? A man dressed in soft clothing? Behold, those who wear soft clothing are in kings' houses. What then did you go out to see? A prophet? Yes, I tell you, and more than a prophet. This is he of whom it is written,
> 'Behold, I send my messenger before your face,
> who will prepare your way before you.'
> Truly, I say to you, among those born of women there has arisen no one greater than John the Baptist. Yet the one who is least in the kingdom of heaven is greater than he. From the days of John the Baptist until now the kingdom of heaven has suffered violence, and the violent take it by force. For all the Prophets and the Law prophesied until John, and if you are willing to accept it, he is Elijah who is to come. He who has ears to hear, let him hear." (Matthew 11:7-15)

Here, to describe John's ministry, our Lord does not quote the Isaiah 40:3 passage, as John did, but rather the words of Malachi 3:1. However, He did not use the words of Malachi 4:5 which specifically name Elijah. So, what, exactly, did our Lord actually mean? What, precisely did He say?

> "If you are willing to accept it, he is the Elijah who was to come. He who has ears, let him hear."

There are two things to note here, before we even start to discuss what is meant by "accept it". The first is the use of the word "if", which makes this statement conditional; in other words, John the Baptist may be Elijah, or he may not be. It depends.[42] It depends upon what? Whether or not you (the Jews of that generation) accepted it (whatever that means).

The second point of note is that Christ followed this statement with the words, "He who has ears, let him hear." That is a Hebraism, a figure of speech, meaning that what had just been said was difficult to understand. Thus, if we have problems understanding precisely what Christ meant, and the exact relationship between John the Baptist and Elijah, we should not be surprised. It is not an easy matter.

So, what was the 'it'? What was it the Jews had to accept? The context makes it clear that the 'it' was the Kingdom of Heaven, and they had to accept 'it' by repenting, for not only was that John's message, it was also Christ's opening clarion call.

> From that time on Jesus began to preach, saying "Repent, for the kingdom of heaven is at hand." (Matthew 4:17)

---

[42] For a discussion on the conditional statements of Christ, see Appendix 4.

Did the Jews as a nation repent? Individuals amongst them did, but as a nation they did not, especially not their leadership. John was beheaded. Christ was crucified. And some of the apostles were executed. That being the case, the 'if', the condition in Christ's statement, was not fulfilled, and John the Baptist was not Elijah! Or was he?

The Transfiguration

We have three accounts of the transfiguration (Matthew 17:1-13; Mark 9:2-14 and Luke 9:28-36) in which the three disciples see a 'vision' of Elijah and Moses. In the KJV we read:

> And as they were coming down from the mountain, Jesus commanded them, saying, "Tell no one the *vision*, until the Son of man is raised from the dead." (Matthew 17:9)

The ESV, KJV and others correctly translate the Greek word *horama* as 'vision' as in Acts 9:10,12 and elsewhere.

Also, in both Matthew's and Mark's account of the Transfiguration we have recorded the disciples' question.

> "Then why do the scribes say that first Elijah must come?" (Matthew 17:10)

In this the scribes, the teachers of the Law (NIV) were not wrong. Not only does it clearly state this in Malachi, but our Lord Jesus Christ confirms that they are correct.

> "Elijah does come, and he will restore all things. But I tell you that Elijah has already come, and they did not recognize him, but did to him whatever they pleased. So

also the Son of Man will certainly suffer at their hands."
(Matthew 17:11-12)

Before commenting upon this, it is interesting to note that the disciples' question and the Lord's answer are omitted from the third Gospel. This is probably because Luke was writing for a Gentile, Theophilus (Luke 1:3), and Elijah and his return is a difficult issue and concerns the people of Israel and their land. However, the Lord's answer to their question "why do the scribes say that first Elijah must come?" was:

> "Behold, I will send you Elijah the prophet before the great and awesome day of the Lord comes. And he will turn the hearts of fathers to their children and the hearts of children to their fathers, lest I come and strike the land with a decree of utter destruction," (Malachi 4:5-6)

Here we read of the land, that is the land of Israel, and also about the great and dreadful day of the Lord; also, the subject of Joel's prophecy which deals with judgment to be inflicted on that land and its people. However, to return to the Lord's answer.

> "Elijah does come, and he will restore all things." (Matthew 17:11)

Yes! Elijah is to come first and will restore all things, says our Lord. No problem with that! But then Christ said:

> "But I tell you that Elijah has already come, and they did not recognize him, but did to him whatever they pleased. So also the Son of Man will certainly suffer at their hands." (Matthew 17:12)

Here we have, seemingly, two contradictions. The first being that earlier the Lord had said:

> "*If* you are willing to accept it, he is Elijah who is to come. He who has ears, let him hear." (Matthew 11:14-15)

This is conditional; note the 'if' and, as we discussed earlier, the conditions were not met and so John the Baptist was not Elijah. However, in Matthew 17:12, there seems to be a direct statement that John the Baptist was Elijah!

The second contradiction is that in Matthew 17:11. There we are told that Elijah is to come and "restore all things" but John the Baptist did not do this! He did not restore all things. He was beheaded; Christ was crucified; some of the apostles were martyred, and later the temple and Jerusalem were destroyed by the Romans. Not only that, the Lord uses the future tense: "To be sure, Elijah comes and *will* restore all things". If the Lord is speaking about Elijah coming in the future, He cannot have been referring to John, but why then does He say that Elijah has already come?

Elijah has already come

Everything we have seen up to now, except for this verse (Matthew 17:12), indicates that John the Baptist was *not* Elijah. He denied it. The Lord, at first, uses the conditional 'if' when linking John and Elijah. John did not restore all things, as Elijah is to do, so John was not Elijah. But then we read, "Elijah has already come".

The problem here is a difficulty in translation. Although Greek has a word for the definite article 'the' (*ho*), it has no word for the indefinite article; i.e. there is no Greek word for 'a' or 'an'. If we turn to Mark 1:6 we find:

Now John was clothed with camel's hair, and wore *a* leather belt around his waist, and ate locusts and wild honey.

However, if we read it in the Greek we would see no "a" before the word for "leather belt". The translators have supplied it to make it good English. Not only is this the case with certain nouns, it is also the case with some expressions. For example, in our Bible we should read 'a' day of the Lord in some places where the translators have put 'the' day of the Lord.[43] And this, according to C. E. McLain in *Elijah's Coming ... and other Neglected Prophecies*, is also the case with names and McLain would translate what our Lord said to His disciples as follows:

> "But I tell you [an] Elijah has already come, and they did not recognise him, but have done to him everything they wished. In the same way the Son of Man is going to suffer at their hands." (Matthew 17:12)

However, Elijah was, and will be, a person, not a generic term or commodity. Thus, the translation "*an* Elijah" may not be possible. But it does seem that what our Lord meant was that John the Baptist was a *type* of Elijah, he was **'an'** Elijah[44], but he was not **'the'** Elijah. This understanding does resolve the apparent contradiction between verses 11 and 12 of Matthew 17, where verse 11 states that Elijah is to come and "will restore all things" and verse 12, where we read "Elijah has already come". It also concurs with what the Angel Gabriel told John's father before his conception, namely,

---

[43] See *The Day of the Lord! When?* by Michael Penny, published by The Open Bible Trust

[44] "An Elijah" is an expression used by Norval Geldenhuys (*The New London Commentary on the New Testament: The Gospel of Luke*, page 65)

that "he will go on before the Lord, *in the spirit and power of Elijah*". This John most certainly did do, but he most definitely did not fulfil all that Malachi, and the Lord Jesus, said Elijah would do.

Appendix 4: Conditional Statements by Christ

There may be some Christians who are surprised, even perturbed, by the fact that our Lord Jesus made conditional, or qualified, statements. However, we have seen that passages like Jeremiah 18:7-10 indicate that some prophecies of blessing and others of judgment were conditional. Similarly, sometimes alternatives are offered (e.g. Isaiah 1:19-20 where 'if' is used twice). And of course, Deuteronomy 28 makes it clear that blessing or judgments would come upon Israel depending on how well they followed the Law and commandments.

Also, as we have seen in the New Testament, in some instances what God said He was to do depended upon what people did. If they repented there would be one course of action; if they did not repent, then a different set of events would follow – similar to Isaiah 1:19-20.

Our Lord Jesus Christ made a number of conditional statements, ones which were qualified, and dependent on other factors. We could say that the outcome of what Christ said is covered by Jeremiah 18:7-10, and that may be a contributing factor, but there is more behind what our Lord said.

Some of what Christ stated has been masked by most translations, either because of the difficulties of translating or because the translators were uncomfortable with Christ making conditional statements. However, in doing this, they have put into Christ's mouth prophecies which did not come about. Consider, for instance, the following three:

"When they persecute you in one town, flee to the next, for truly, I say to you, you will not have gone through all the towns of Israel before the Son of Man comes." (Matthew 10:23)

And he said to them, "Truly, I say to you, there are some standing here who will not taste death until they see the kingdom of God after it has come *with power*." (Mark 9:1: Luke 9:27; see also Matthew 16:28)

"From the fig tree learn its lesson: as soon as its branch becomes tender and puts out its leaves, you know that summer is near. So also, when you see all these things, you know that he is near, at the very gates. Truly, I say to you, this generation will not pass away until all these things take place. Heaven and earth will pass away, but my words will not pass away." (Matthew 24:32-35; see also Luke 21:29-33)

Now all three of these passages, in the English, have Christ making an unequivocal statement, yet what Christ said would happen did **not** actually happen! In other words, they did finish going through the cities of Israel and Christ did not return. They all died and the Kingdom of God did not come in with power. And although *some* of the events described in Matthew 24 happened before that generation died out, not **all** of them did. So did Christ make false statements? No! In the Greek His statements are *conditional*. The Greek does not say something "will" *definitely* happen, but that something "may" happen; it might.

The problem lies in the Greek language. The above passages all have the two Greek words *eos an*, which make the statements conditional. Some translations do attempt to translate this particle, wanting to show that what the Lord said was a possibility, rather than a certainty. *Young's Literal Translation* uses the word 'may' and the *Westcott and Hort Interlinear* uses 'might'. In the following quotations, the italics and bold italics are mine, and are not in the original.

Matthew 10:23

W&H	But whenever they persecute you in the city, be fleeing to a different one. For amen I am saying to you, you *might* not not complete the cities of Israel until the Son of Man *might* come.
Young's	And whenever they may persecute you in this city, flee to the other, for verily I say to you, ye *may* not have completed the cities of Israel till the Son of Man *may* come.

Matthew 16:28

W&H	Amen I am saying to you, some of the ones standing here *might* not not taste death until *likely* (Gr *an*) they *might* see the Son of Man coming in the Kingdom of Him.
Young's	Verily I say to you, there are certain of those standing here who shall not taste of death till they *may* see the Son of Man coming in his reign.

Matthew 24:34

W&H	Amen I am saying to you, this generation should not not *likely* (Gr. *an*) pass away until all these things should occur.
Young's	Verily I say to you, this generation *may* not pass away till all these *may* come to pass.

Mark 9:1

W&H	And He was saying to them, Amen I am saying to you that some of the ones having stood here should not not taste of death until *likely* (Gr. *an*) they *might* see the kingdom of God coming in power.
Young's	And he said to them, 'Verily I say to you, That there are certain of those standing here, who *may* not taste of death till they see the reign of God having come in power.'

Luke 9:27

W&H	Truthfully I am saying to you some of the ones who having stood here should not not taste death until *likely* (Gr. *an*) they should see the kingdom of God.
Young's	and I say to you, truly, there are certain of those here standing, who shall not taste of death till they *may* see the reign of God.'

Although Robert Young introduced "may", his translation is cumbersome and unclear in English, and many find the Westcott and Hort one even more so, especially their use of "not not"!

As mentioned, the main problem lies in the original language and the two Greek words *eos an*, which have been translated "until" or "before" in the *NIV* or "till" in the *KJV*. The notes of *The Companion Bible* on these verses are helpful.

> Matthew 16:28 till = the particle *an*, with the Subjunctive Mood, gives this a hypothetical force.

Matthew 24:34 till = here with the Greek *an*, and the subjunctive mood, marking the uncertainty which was conditional on the repentance of Israel.

Mark 9:1 till = Greek *eos an*. The particle *an* makes this clause conditional; the condition being the repentance of the nation [of Israel at the call of Peter. Acts 3:19-26; cp. Acts 28:25-27.]

Luke 21:32 till all be fulfilled = till (Greek *eos an*) all may possibly come to pass ... Had the nation repented at Peter's call in Acts 2:38; 3:19-26 "all that the prophets had spoken" would have come to pass.

Most translations of these verses imply the prophecies were very definite statements, seemingly stating categorically that something was going to be fulfilled within a relatively short space of time. However, this is not what the Greek infers. According to the above notes from *The Companion Bible*, the use of *eos an* with the subjunctive mood renders such prophecies hypothetical, possible, conditional. That those events prophesied will happen sometime is certain, but of them happening within the short time period specified depended on specific conditions being met. If those conditions were met, then the events would follow soon. If the conditions were not met, then the events would not follow soon. This is precisely what Walter Bauer states in *A Greek-English Lexicon of the New Testament and Other Early Christian Literature* of this Greek word *an*.

A particle peculiar to Greek, incapable of translation by a single word; it denotes that the action of the verb is dependent on some circumstance or condition.

We may paraphrase these verses as follows:

> "When you are persecuted in one place, flee to another. I tell you the truth, [it is possible that] you will not finish going through the cities of Israel before the Son of Man comes." (Matthew 10:23)

> And he said to them, "I tell you the truth, [it is possible that] some who are standing here will not taste death before they see the Kingdom of God come *with power*." (Mark 9:1: Luke 9:27; also Matthew 16:28)

> "Now learn this lesson from the fig tree: As soon as its twigs get tender and its leaves come out, you know that summer is near. Even so, when you see all these things, you know that it is near, right at the door. I tell you the truth, [it is possible that] this generation will certainly not pass away until all these things have happened. Heaven and earth will pass away, but my words will never pass away." (Matthew 24:32-35; see also Luke 21:29-33)

[For more on these verses and the difficulty of translating *eos an*; see Michael Penny's *40 Problem Passage*, number 12, available from The Open Bible Trust.]

Appendix 5:
More on Elijah

Christ on the Cross

> And about the ninth hour Jesus cried out with a loud voice, saying, "*Eli, Eli, lema sabachthani?*" that is, "My God, my God, why have you forsaken me?" And some of the bystanders, hearing it, said, "This man is calling Elijah." And one of them at once ran and took a sponge, filled it with sour wine, and put it on a reed and gave it to him to drink. But the others said, "Wait, let us see whether Elijah will come to save him." (Matthew 27:46-49)

> And at the ninth hour Jesus cried with a loud voice, "*Eloi, Eloi, lema sabachthani?*" which means, "My God, my God, why have you forsaken me?" And some of the bystanders hearing it said, "Behold, he is calling Elijah." And someone ran and filled a sponge with sour wine, put it on a reed and gave it to him to drink, saying, "Wait, let us see whether Elijah will come to take him down." (Mark 15:34-36)

Here we see how the Jews were looking for Elijah, and note how Luke leaves this part out of his gospel. Maybe the Jews of 2,000 years ago were concentrating so hard on looking for Elijah that they missed their Messiah, but maybe some Gentile Christians today are looking so hard for the second coming of Christ that they will miss the return of Elijah, which is to precede it.

The Two Witnesses of Revelation! Is one Elijah?

Revelation is a difficult book to understand, but there is one passage which may allude to Elijah. It refers to the land of Israel, the city of Jerusalem and the temple.

> Then I was given a measuring rod like a staff, and I was told, "Rise and measure the temple of God and the altar and those who worship there, but do not measure the court outside the temple; leave that out, for it is given over to the nations, and they will trample the holy city for forty-two months. And I will grant authority to my two witnesses, and they will prophesy for 1,260 days, clothed in sackcloth."
>
> These are the two olive trees and the two lampstands that stand before the Lord of the earth. And if anyone would harm them, fire pours from their mouth and consumes their foes. If anyone would harm them, this is how he is doomed to be killed. They have the power to shut the sky, that no rain may fall during the days of their prophesying, and they have power over the waters to turn them into blood and to strike the earth with every kind of plague, as often as they desire. And when they have finished their testimony, the beast that rises from the bottomless pit will make war on them and conquer them and kill them, and their dead bodies will lie in the street of the great city that symbolically is called Sodom and Egypt, where their Lord was crucified. For three and a half days some from the peoples and tribes and languages and nations will gaze at their dead bodies and refuse to let them be placed in a tomb, and those who dwell on the earth will rejoice over them and make merry and exchange presents, because these two prophets had been a torment to those who

dwell on the earth. But after the three and a half days a breath of life from God entered them, and they stood up on their feet, and great fear fell on those who saw them. Then they heard a loud voice from heaven saying to them, "Come up here!" And they went up to heaven in a cloud, and their enemies watched them. And at that hour there was a great earthquake, and a tenth of the city fell. Seven thousand people were killed in the earthquake, and the rest were terrified and gave glory to the God of heaven. (Revelation 11:1-13)

I do not wish to get involved in the detailed interpretation of this passage but a number of commentators suggest that one of these two witnesses will be Elijah. Possible reasons for this being so is that the passage speaks of:

1) Fire from heaven, and
2) The power to shut up the sky so that it will not rain during the time they are prophesying.

Both of these were significant miracles in the ministry of Elijah. First, in his battle with the prophets of the false god Baal, Elijah was vindicated by fire from heaven.

And at the time of the offering of the oblation, Elijah the prophet came near and said, "O Lord, God of Abraham, Isaac, and Israel, let it be known this day that you are God in Israel, and that I am your servant, and that I have done all these things at your word. Answer me, O Lord, answer me, that this people may know that you, O Lord, are God, and that you have turned their hearts back." Then the fire of the Lord fell and consumed the burnt offering and the wood and the stones and the dust, and licked up the water that was in the trench. (1 Kings 18:36-38)

Read the whole of 1 Kings 18 for the full account, which also mentions the end of the drought, an event referred to by James in his letter.

> Elijah was a man with a nature like ours, and he prayed fervently that it might not rain, and for three years and six months it did not rain on the earth. Then he prayed again, and heaven gave rain, and the earth bore its fruit. (James 5:17-18)

The events mentioned in Revelation 11:1-14 take place over a period of 42 months, or 1260 days. This refers to the 3½ years just prior to the Lord's return; also described as the time of Jacob's troubles, the great tribulation and the Day of the Lord. Thus if Elijah is to be around at that time, then he must also be around for some time prior to that. When will he first appear on the scene? And what is he to do?

The Return of Elijah

The Bible is silent as to when Elijah will return, but it does tell us what he is to do. And also, by considering other similar situations and events in the Bible, we may be able to draw some parallels.

Today, many Gentile Christians teach all prophecy relating to Israel has been fulfilled and that God has completely finished with Israel as a special nation before Him. Part of the reason for this is that some find it difficult to envisage how God would go about re-establishing the Jewish priesthood, temple, sacrifices, etc.

However, there are two situations in the Bible which may shed some light on this predicament.

Following the reign of Solomon civil war broke out in Israel and the nation was split in two; the northern ten tribes (called Israel) and the southern two tribes (called Judah). First the Assyrians captured the northern ten tribes, and then, later, the Babylonians under Nebuchadnezzar conquered the two southern tribes, razing both Jerusalem and the temple to the ground. After seventy years in exile, the Medo-Persians conquered the Babylonians, and some of the Jews returned and started to rebuild Jerusalem, its walls, and the temple. However, there were certain things they could not do. For example, we read:

> The governor told them that they were not to partake of the most holy food, until there should be a priest to consult with Urim and Thummim. (Ezra 2:63; see also Nehemiah 7:65)

The Urim and Thummim were two stones which were placed in the priest's garments and used to cast lots. Probably one said "Yes" and the other "No". In this way the Israelites were able to ascertain the will of God on a particular matter, as with the selection of John the Baptist's father, Zechariah, to burn incense in the temple; (Luke 1:8-9; see also Exodus 28:30; Numbers 27:21; 1 Chronicles 24:5,31; and see also chapter 'The Casting of Lots' in *The Miracles of the Apostles* by Michael Penny, published by The Open Bible Trust: page 68 details.) Thus a period without temple worship was brought to an end by a priest using Urim and Thummim.

The other example follows the 400 years of silence, from the words of Malachi at the end of the Old Testament to the start of the New. There were private angelic visitations to Zechariah, Mary and Joseph; two miraculous births; a special star; but then another 30 years of silence. Silence until a voice cried in the wilderness, "Repent, for the kingdom of heaven is near!"

This is the situation Israel finds itself in today. There has been a long period of silence from God. There has been no temple worship since AD 70. How is all this going to end? We may never know, and even when it does end, the Gentile world may well not be aware of it. For example, were any in Persia aware that in Israel a priest with Urim and Thummim had come onto the scene? Was it reported to the Roman Governor of Israel, let alone the Caesar in Rome, that John the Baptist had started preaching? Thus when Elijah returns and starts his work of restoration in Israel, it is doubtful if *The Times*, the *BBC*, or any of the world's media will report it, even if they become aware of it. Thus unlike the Lord's second coming, which will be with power and great glory, on the clouds of heaven, with accompanying earthquakes, Elijah's return is likely to be quiet, and insignificant to the Gentile world. However, that may change when his work of restoration is underway.

Restoration of all things

An important word, and work, in all this is 'restore'. It comes in a number of significant passages. First of all, Peter urged the people of Israel (Acts 3:12) to....

> "Repent therefore, and turn again, that your sins may be blotted out, that times of refreshing may come from the presence of the Lord, and that he may send the Christ appointed for you, Jesus, whom heaven must receive until the time for restoring all the things about which God spoke by the mouth of his holy prophets long ago." (Acts 3:19-21)

Here we are told that Christ must remain in heaven until the time comes for God to 'restore' everything. Gentile Christians are prone to think that it is Christ Himself, when He comes, who will 'restore' everything, but that is not the situation. Christ, Himself, said:

> "Elijah does come and he will *restore* all things." (Matthew 17:11)

> "Elijah does come first, to *restore* all things." (Mark 9:12)

So Elijah is to come first, before the Lord returns, and restore all things, but what is it that Elijah is to restore?

> "Behold, I will send you Elijah the prophet before the great and awesome day of the Lord comes. And he will turn the hearts of fathers to their children and the hearts of children to their fathers, lest I come and strike the land with a decree of utter destruction." (Malachi 4:5-6)

One of the things Elijah is to restore amongst the people of Israel is family relationships; thus reversing Micah 7:6, which Christ quotes in Matthew 10:35-36.

> "For I have come to set a man against his father, and a daughter against her mother, and a daughter-in-law against her mother-in-law. And a person's enemies will be those of his own household."

But there is more for Elijah to restore.

> "Behold, I send my messenger, and he will prepare the way before me. And the Lord whom you seek will suddenly come to his temple; and the messenger of the covenant in

whom you delight, behold, he is coming, says the Lord of hosts. But who can endure the day of his coming, and who can stand when he appears? For he is like a refiner's fire and like fullers' soap. He will sit as a refiner and purifier of silver, and he will purify the sons of Levi and refine them like gold and silver, and they will bring offerings in righteousness to the Lord. Then the offering of Judah and Jerusalem will be pleasing to the Lord as in the days of old and as in former years." (Malachi 3:1-4)

If this passage is also referring to Elijah, then we see that a temple and offerings need to be restored. "This cannot be!" shouts the Gentile Christian, but are Gentiles correct in such protest? For example, during the time covered by the Acts of the Apostles it was right and proper for Jewish Christians to continue to follow the Law of Moses, and we can see this in Acts where they kept the Sabbath, attended the temple on feast days, circumcised their male children, took Nazirite vows, shaved their heads, made offerings etc. If the Jewish Christians had not continued doing all of these things, then those Jews who had not yet come to believe in the Lord Jesus as their Christ and the Son of God, would simply not have listened to the Jewish Christians. Not only that, they would have had nothing to do with them, terming them "Gentile dogs!"

Also the Jewish sacrifices achieved nothing for, as Hebrews 10:4 puts it, "It is impossible for the blood of bulls and goats to take away sins." The value of animal sacrifices was in teaching. They were types, in that they foreshadowed Christ's one sacrifice for sin, but in themselves they could not be efficacious. Thus if Elijah is to restore the temple with its offerings, Gentile Christians have no theological grounds for complaint. It may well be the way God is going to teach the Jews that Christ died for their sins; that His sacrifice is the one which takes away sins; that He was the Lamb of God who took away the sin of the world.

Also we need to realise why, after the risen Lord had taught the disciples for 40 days after His resurrection, after he had "opened their minds so they could understand the Scriptures" (Luke 24:45), the last question they asked Him before he ascended into heaven was:

> "Lord, will you at this time restore the kingdom to Israel?" (Acts 1:6)

And His reply was:

> "It is not for you to know times or seasons that the Father has fixed by his own authority." (1:7)

If God is *never* going to restore the kingdom to Israel because they had crucified their Messiah, as some Gentile Christians state, then here was the golden opportunity for Him to say so, but He did not. Again, we have an evasive answer: "It's not for you to know!" Why not? Because it depends! As He said earlier:

> "*If* you are willing to accept it, he is Elijah who is to come. He who has ears, let him hear." (Matthew 11:14-15)

If they were willing to accept it, the 'it' was repentance, then the kingdom of heaven, which was near, would soon have followed, as we saw earlier, and the kingdom would have been restored to Israel. And even after His death and glorious resurrection it was still a possibility and repentance was still the key, as Peter made clear in Acts 3:19-21:

"Repent therefore … [so] that your sins may be blotted out … [so] that times of refreshing may come from the presence of the Lord ... [so] that he may send the Christ appointed for you, Jesus, whom heaven must receive until the time for restoring all the things about which God spoke by the mouth of his holy prophets long ago."

If Israel, as a nation, had repented, their sins would have been wiped away, the times of refreshing would have come in, the kingdom would have been restored to Israel, and Christ would have returned. However, they did not repent as a nation, although some individual Jews did, and so none of that happened. What could have happened in the past, is now to happen sometime in the future, and it is all to begin with the return of Elijah[45], whose opening words to the people of Israel could well be those of John the Baptist and our Lord,

"Repent, for the kingdom of heaven is near."

---

[45] See *Elijah's Coming ... and other Neglected Prophecies* by C E McLain

Peter, Paul, James and John

If you have found this book on John the Baptist of interest then you may care to read one of the following written by Michael Penny.

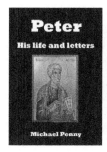 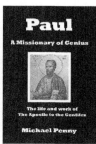 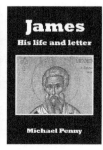 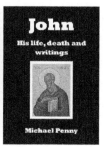

Peter: His life and letters

Paul: A Missionary of Genius
The life and work of The Apostle to the Gentiles

James: His life and letter

John: His life, death and writings

Details of these books can be seen on **www.obt.org.uk**

They can be ordered from that website and from
The Open Bible Trust
Fordland Mount, Upper Basildon,
Reading, RG8 8LU, UK.

They are also available as eBooks from Apple and Amazon
and as paperbacks from Amazon.

About the author

 Michael Penny was born in Ebbw Vale, Wales in 1943. He read Mathematics at the University of Reading before entering teaching and becoming the Director of Mathematics and Business Studies at Queen Mary's College Basingstoke in Hampshire, England. In 1978 he entered Christian publishing, and in 1984 became the administrator of the Open Bible Trust, a position he held for seven years, before moving to the USA and becoming pastor of Grace Church in New Berlin, Wisconsin. He returned to Britain in 1999 and at present he is the editor and administrator of the Open Bible Trust and has written many books and numerous study booklets.

He has been the chair of Churches Together in Reading for ten years and in 2019 was elected chair of Churches Together in Berkshire. He has also been on the Advisory Committee to Reading University Christian Union for nine years. He is lead chaplain at Reading College and is Head Chaplain for Activate Learning Colleges including the City of Oxford College, Banbury College, Blackbird Leys College, Bracknell and Wokingham College, and those in Guildford. He has appeared on Premier Radio and BBC Radio Berks on many occasions. He has an itinerant ministry which takes him into churches of different denominations, mainly in Berkshire and South Oxfordshire.

In 2019 the Bishop of Reading nominated him to receive the Maundy Money from the Queen for his services to Christianity, the Church and the Community. He was one of the 93 men selected by

Buckingham Palace from across the United Kingdom, along with 93 women.

Some of Michael Penny's other major works include

40 Problem Passages
Approaching the Bible
The Bible: myth or message?
Galatians: Interpretation and Application
Joel's Prophecy: Past and Present
The Miracles of the Apostles
Comments and Queries about Christianity
Comments and Queries about the New Testament
Following Philippians (with William Henry)
Introducing God's Plan (with Sylvia Penny)

He has also written many Bible Study Booklets,
as well as a number of study guides including:

Moving through Mark
Learning from Luke
The Manual on the Gospel of John
Going through Galatians
Exploring Ephesians
A Study Guide to Psalm 119
The Purpose of Parables
The Balanced Christian Life (Ephesians)
Search the Acts of the Apostles (with Neville Stephens)

For details of the above, please visit **www.obt.org.uk**

They are available as eBooks from Apple and Amazon
and as paperbacks from Amazon.

Free Magazine

Michael Penny is editor of *Search* magazine.

For a free sample of
the Open Bible Trust's magazine *Search*, please email

admin@obt.org.uk

or visit

www.obt.org.uk/search

Index of Subjects

Bibliography of Books Quoted or Referred to

Barclay, William: The Daily Study Bible; The Gospel of Matthew 64,74

Baur, Walter: A Greek-English Lexicon of the New Testament and Other Early Christian Literature   124

Berry, George Ricker: Interlinear Greek-Hebrew New Testament 33

Bullinger, E W: A Critical Lexicon and Concordance   45

Bullinger, E W: The Companion Bible   30,62,123

Geldenhuys, Norval: The New London Commentary: The Gospel of Luke   12,24,116

Ginn, Roy: Nicodemus: Understanding 'Being born again'   98

Gooding, David: According to Luke   27

Henry, W M: The Speeches in Acts   90

Hill, David: The New Century Bible Commentary; The Gospel of Matthew   29,64

Josephus: Antiquities of the Jews   57,69,71,72,105

Josephus: The Life of Josephus   22

Lietzmann, Hans: Beginning of the Christian Church   32

Marsh, John: Saint John   43

McLain, C E: Elijah's Coming ... and other Neglected Prophecies 134

Penny, Michael: Daniel's Seventy Sevens: A Recalculation   9

Penny, Michael: 40 Problem Passages   124

Penny, Michael: A Key to Unfulfilled Prophecy: Jeremiah 18:7-10 102

Penny, Michael: Deuteronomy 28: A Key to Understanding   6,102

Penny, Michael: John: His life, death and writing   38

Penny, Michael: Paul: A Missionary of Genius   90

****

Printed in Great Britain
by Amazon

77902583R00081